Praise for Feature

"Working with Charlotte I have developed stronger professional and personal boundaries. She is a very down-to-earth teacher and healer who I've followed through her example. I am a better person because of her! The future guest of the Oprah show......thanks Char for all you do & have done for me!"

— LORI JONES, Massage Therapist and Trainer

"Latif has been my realtor and a friend for the past 15 years. His loyalty, dedication, knowledge and understanding of the housing market is truly remarkable. He is the best of the best. Latif is trustworthy, honest and my realtor for life!"

— MARC SCAGLIONE, President, Park West Gallery

"Anna Russo is one of the most knowledgeable NLP Trainers and Life Coaches I have come across. I trust her professionally as well as personally. I am impressed with the way she helps people create changes quickly and easily. I recommend her training to anybody that wants to live at their full potential."

— MIKE BRIDGES, G.M. / ABB, Inc., Auburn Hills, MI

"Dr. Jane Stewart puts a new spin on the way to achieve peak mental performance. Challenges don't have to stand in the way."

—PATRICIA PEARSON, MA, CI, CEO Harbor Center

"Profound, simple, and effective, I found Gail & Louis' Referral Networking system & Strategic Thinking Process (STP) to be truly a blueprint any business owner could follow when they are ready to deepen their relationships with key contacts and survive tough economic times. This is truly a roadmap to business success."

— JOHNNY "THE TRANSITION MAN" CAMPBELL, DTM, AS Change & Generational Marketing Expert.

"PC Miracles has been doing our IT work for years. We were very happy when PC Miracles released the "Effort Free IT Platinum" plan. We had been asking them to provide this type of service and we are very happy with how it's worked out. We are able to predict most of our IT costs for the year. With the "Effort Free IT - Platinum" plan we have also received faster response times to our issues. When we do have an issue, after business hours, they know about it before we do and they have a technician addressing the critical issues the very next morning. We have also seen a reduction in downtime since being on the "Effort Free IT - Platinum" plan."

— JULIE JOHNSON, Owner Acclaim Legal Services

"When we had problems with our balance sheet, Marie Jakubiak was able to identify the issue quickly and put our minds at ease. She is an honest and hard working person and has always been available to us. I would encourage anyone who is in need of CPA services to work with Marie."

— RENEE SIEGEL, Tri-County Floor Covering, Inc.

30 DAY

TOTAL BUSINESS

MAKEOVER

Minesh Baxi and Associates LLC
Troy, MI

Printed in the United States of America.

ISBN: 978-0-9790322-3-3

Acknowledgements

I want to acknowledge three groups of people:

1. The contributing authors of this book who went outside their comfort zones and have generously provided valuable expertise for the reader.
2. My wife who has been a great support and my wonderful children Mooskaan and Saahil for being the inspiration. I have also received great support and encouragement from Kim's family especially her mother and her sister, Margaret.
3. The team who helped us complete the book project includes: Kathi Dunn, Tove Baessler, Tressa Foster, Tonya Shirelle and others.

Minesh Baxi, *Publisher*

Contents

Part One: Vision and Goal Setting Makeover

1. What Separates Wealthy and Successful People – MINESH BAXI...3

2. The Secret To Tapping Into Your Passion – CHARLOTTE IRWIN 5

3. If You Can Believe It, You Can Achieve It – RICK MAROSE AND RENE DECHERT 10

4. The Joys And Sorrows Of A Serial Entrepreneur – LATIF MUHAIMEEN 15

5. How To Design Your Future – NLP Strategies That Work – ANNA RUSSO...22

6. Brain Fitness – The Secret To Peak Mental Performance – JANE STEWART, PH.D. 30

7. Create A Simple, Single Page Business Plan – AMY GROSSMAN...37

8. Don't Be An Average Joe Business Owner: Start With The End In Mind – MARISA PETRELLA, ATTORNEY AT LAW 42

9. Achieve Financial Freedom By Building And Selling Your Company – JEFF WRIGHT...51

10. Will You Get The Paycheck You Deserve? 5 Things You Can Do To Maximize Your Exit Strategy – RICK SMITH.......................57

Part Two: Marketing And Sales Makeover

11. Get The Competitive Edge By Raising Your Price – DR. BRYAN CORNWALL...65

12. Publicity: Find a True P.R. Angle And Get Promoted For Free – LISA LAPIDES SAWICKI...70

13. Marketer Of Marketing Shares Exclusive Marketing Secrets
    – Pete Swartz..76

14. Confused Prospects Never Buy – Dr. Scott McLeod...........81

15. Ten Ways To Add Sex Appeal To Your Business
    – Todd Gulich 87

16. The Referral Miracle: The Fable of the Magical Coins
    – Charles Gifford..94

17. Seven Matchmaking Tips for Finding, Dating,
    and Keeping Business Referral Partners
    – Gail Michelman and Louis Weiss 98

18. Who Do I Know Strategy.... Who You Want To Know
    & Why – Natalie DeLeo..104

19. When to Pop The Question? Timing The Close
    – Minesh Baxi..111

20. 5 Keys To Match Your Business Goals To Your Website
    – Steve Hyer...117

21. Building Your Business Brand Using Audio, Web Video
    and Automated Sales Funnels – Ted Cantu.......................122

Part Three: Leadership and Management Makeover

22. Why Should You Be A Leader? – Susan West.......................131

23. Break Through YOUR Income Ceiling In 8 Simple Steps
    – Mary Dunlap 135

24. Don't Be The Gopher, Be The Executive
    – Gary Pipia and Minesh Baxi..143

25. 15 Steps To Retaining Your Best Employees
    – T. Varatha Rajan 149

26. How To Make Sure Your Computer Consultant Is An
    Asset To Your Company And Not A Liability!
    – Dan Izydorek 156

Part Four: Financial and Risk Prevention Makeover

27. Use Your CPA To Give Yourself Peace Of Mind
   – Marie A. Jakubiak, CPA 167

28. The 3-Step Financial Makeover
   – Todd Rammler, CMA, MSA....................................173

29. Maximize The Benefits of Your Business And Minimize Your
   Exposure – Eric Gould, JD, LLM (Taxation) 180

30. Your Free Cup Of Coffee, A Gas Card And 3 Questions You
   Must Ask Before Buying Insurance – Sharon Barnes 185

31. The HSA: An Innovative Yet Simple Method, Guaranteed To
   Reduce Your Personal Health Care Cost – Keith Parke 190

32. Why Your Father's Retirement Plan Won't Work For You
   – Sandra Wright with Minesh Baxi 199

33. A Contingency Plan – The "Do Or Die" Safety Net For Business
   Owners – Pat Byrd 206

34. What's The Enemy: Spending More Or Spending
   Less On Employee Benefits – Ted Himelhoch
   And Martyn Dickinson 213

35. Bonus Section: Makeover Success Stories from
   Chambers/Associations:....................................220
   – Jennifer Kluge, *Michigan Business Owners and Professionals Association*
   – Sheri Heiney, *Rochester Regional Chamber of Commerce*
   – Penny Shanks, *Clarkston Area Chamber of Commerce*
   – Marie Hauswirth, *Waterford Area Chamber of Commerce*
   – Mailè Ilac Boeder, *Ferndale Chamber of Commerce*

PART ONE
Vision and Goal Setting Makeover

What Separates Wealthy and Successful People
MINESH BAXI

The Secret To Tapping Into Your Passion
CHARLOTTE IRWIN

If You Can Believe It, You Can Achieve It
RICK MAROSE AND RENE DECHERT

The Joys And Sorrows Of A Serial Entrepreneur
LATIF MUHAIMEEN

How To Design Your Future - NLP Strategies That Work
ANNA RUSSO

Brain Fitness – The Secret To Peak Mental Performance
JANE STEWART, PH.D.

Create A Simple, Single Page Business Plan
AMY GROSSMAN

Don't Be An Average Joe Business Owner: Start With The End In Mind
MARISA PETRELLA, ATTORNEY AT LAW

Achieve Financial Freedom By Building And Selling Your Company
JEFF WRIGHT

Will You Get The Paycheck You Deserve?
5 Things You Can Do To Maximize Your Exit Strategy
RICK SMITH

What Separates Wealthy And Successful People

By Minesh Baxi

Thanks for picking up this book! As the publisher of the book, I am grateful that you found this book interesting and worthwhile enough to start reading it.

Let me start with the conversation I had with one of my clients. This client is a wealthy investor and he is also a savvy business owner. We were discussing what separates wealthy and successful people from those who are not.

Do you know what that one thing is? It is really simple yet quite profound.

Wealthy and successful people actively seek counsel and advice specific to their goals!

The question then becomes – who is your mentor? If you have a mentor or a coach who is helping you create and implement strategies then you are on your way to achieving your goals.

If you do not have a mentor then your chances of achieving success become diminished.

My mentor was the main reason I was able to successfully publish my first book after numerous failed attempts.

Why read this book?

This book has been put together with one key goal in mind and that is to provide you with ideas from different experts to assist you in getting the results you want. The book covers ideas relating to setting your goals and writing a business plan to marketing techniques to attract clients offline and online. There are more ideas to help you with managing your finances and also becoming a better leader.

Here is my challenge to you. Read one chapter a day and implement just one idea from that chapter. In 30 days, we have actually more than 30 chapters, you will have totally transformed your business.

If you don't feel like you can do it by yourself, hire one of the experts featured in the book to help you take the idea to completion.

Have you ever thought of writing a book?

Here are three questions every prospect is asking:

a. Why should I buy the product or services you are selling?
b. Why should I buy them from YOU?
c. Why should I buy NOW?

If you do not have clear answers to all these three questions, it is unlikely that your message will be heard amidst the noise and more importantly, your prospect will not make the buying decision in your favor.

I started writing books so I could educate my prospects by answering these three questions. If you have not created information products to assist you in getting your message through to your prospects, I encourage that you start now.

Call or email me to get the Audio CD free – *"7 **Ways To Be Recognized As An Expert"*** and you can get started on your journey to creating effective marketing tools to attract more clients.

Thanks again for reading this book. Enjoy.

minesh@mbaxi.com

877-968-2500

The Secret To Tapping Into Your Passion
By Charlotte Irwin

First of all, I want to thank you for having the vision and a desire to be on your own.

I am sure you are aware that a number of people are leading confused lives. It is apparent from the dull, meaningless and empty existence they have. Some choose to live vicariously watching insipid reality shows and others waste their resources pursuing happiness in the form of drugs, alcohol and other forms of escape.

Obviously you are special because you have the courage to have your own business, a way to add value to other people's lives. Yet do you ever question your purpose? Do you feel like you are running out of steam? Do you end the day wondering how long you can continue on this journey? Are tough times draining your spirit and drive?

If you are asking any of these questions, it is time to ask yourself – am I truly leading a purposeful life?

You may ask: how will I know that I am leading a purposeful life?

Let me tell you a little bit about me and my life.

I clearly remember that moment -the feeling of being scared. I knew I had discovered my purpose in life and I also knew to fulfill it I needed to make a huge shift from a successful career with a large corporation to starting a business whose purpose mirrored my life's purpose.

Mostly I was afraid I would lose my comfortable lifestyle. As the saying goes, I felt the fear and did it anyway. I know now it was about knowing my purpose, igniting my passion about it and persevering in the journey. In a few years, I built a very successful business with over half a million in revenue each year.

At this moment you may be wondering, what does this have to do with success in your business?

Let me share with you my experiences during this journey when at times I did question myself but an inner voice guided me and always brought that strength so tough times never seemed to last and always a miraculous path appeared in the wilderness.

At the time when a number of people who appeared much more successful fell by the wayside, Center for Healing Arts and Massage prospered and now has become the biggest massage therapy clinic of its type in the entire state of Michigan.

My most important challenge was how to change my mind. I had formed many limiting beliefs about myself.

I had to practice positive affirmations every day to change the old patterns my mind was familiar with.

I continuously seek resources to support my new beliefs. I attend workshops, listen to CDs, read books and associate only with positive people who align themselves with my new found beliefs.

When things are challenging in a business it is easy to fall back with

- I don't deserve to be rich
- I can't do this
- I'm sick and tired
- I know something will go wrong

Sounds familiar?

Now I change my thoughts to

- How can I grow?
- What does this look like?
- How can I make it better?
- What exciting thing will happen today?
- Who can I call for help?

All these questions result in action steps I can take to resolve any challenge I am having.

Why is it important to know?

Purpose is the difference between:

- Earning a living and *designing a life*
- Achieving goals and *achieving the right goals*
- Just getting by and *leaving your mark*
- Short-lived satisfaction and *lifetime fulfillment*

If you have a firm, clear focus on what your purpose is, you can hang in there when the going gets tough. When sales are down, when people leave, when you lose your motivation, when the economy changes....all these things can interrupt or impact business flow and revenue. However, having a definite purpose will keep you on track and keep your business moving forward. When you have defined your purpose you will see these external events and use them to explore, adjust and realign instead of disasters or misfortune.

Your purpose gives meaning to your life:
- It establishes your unique place in the universe
- It gives you the reason for being and doing, even when all other reasons fail
- It evokes your high sense of being
- It allows you to design your destiny
- It gives purpose to other activities that support your life purpose
- It unifies your values and beliefs

Your purpose can change you and you can change your purpose. It is a function of growth (emotional, spiritually, and intellectual) and is evolutionary.
Your purpose empowers you to focus on resources, time, energy, money, relationships that support your purpose.

The clarity of your purpose allows you to become effective in carrying out your purpose:
- Minimizing the waste and ineffective use of resources
- Attracting the right resources into your life
- Allows you to live with minimum stress, maximum satisfaction and fulfillment of your distinctive style

Your Purpose Gives Perseverance to Your Passion
- Provides Satisfaction for the short term
- Provides Fulfillment for the Long Term
- Provides power to make the runs

Your Purpose gives Your Life Power

This clarity of purpose gives power to all aspects of your life, your work leisure, interest, goals and actions

There are three simple steps in discovering your purpose and truly it is a discovery as nobody can give it to you. It is inside of you but you have to be willing to let the light shine inwards to tap into the guiding light which will emanate from your being to others.

1. Get in touch with your inner self by simply acknowledging your strengths and weaknesses. By truly being in touch with your feelings, you will have the energy to align your thoughts, emotions and values with the purpose in your life.

   Some use meditation and some simply use a journal to record their secret thoughts and wishes so they can realize who they are.

2. Discover what excites you. If it is shopping you may want to turn your passion into having a retail store. If talking to people, helping people excites you, you may want to become a trainer or coach.

   Do you get excited by children and caring for them? You may want to open a day care center or child's play arena. Take the first step by discovering what it is and how you could mesh that into a business

   This is also the time to discover whether your current business or career is truly aligned with what excites you and energizes your passion. You don't have to change your entire business. You could find ways to support your purpose by engaging in activities and organizations who have similar values and are performing the tasks that you alone may fail to accomplish.

3. Take the first step. Life is a journey, so is a business. Don't be afraid to take the first step even if you are not sure that it is your purpose. Like life, business is only a series of experiences that help refine our purpose. Start with something. You may start off thinking you know what it is, but other opportunities may unfold that may be even more exciting. Don't be afraid to experience all of what life has to offer.

About Purpose:

What really is your Life purpose? We all have a unique gift we bring to the world that no one else has or can do. This means you can do it better than 100,000 other people. Did you come to inspire or teach others? Did you come to bring your humor or joy?

What is your business purpose? How do they fit together? Are they in conflict or do they mesh? You may have a moving company but your core business purpose may be more about helping people feel safe and secure about making transitions in their lives. Or like me, I have a massage therapy company to reduce stress in people's lives or more importantly to reinstitute the power of human touch in a culture that has become impersonal and technologically overloaded.

It's a question that takes a great deal of reflection but well worth the effort. Most people never even think about it. When we know our personal purpose and integrate it with our business purpose we become unstoppable to what we can create.

It is the difference between asking, "What has my life been about?" and shouting, *"I have been about my life!"*

> *Working with Charlotte I have developed stronger professional and personal boundaries. She is a very down-to-earth teacher and healer who I've followed through her example. I am a better person because of her! The future guest of the Oprah show......thanks Char for all you do & have done for me!*
> —LORI JONES, Massage Therapist and Trainer

About The Author:

Charlotte Irwin, Owner of the Center for the Healing Arts & Massage, Largest Provider of Massage Therapy in Michigan (www. center4thehealingarts.com) and author of *Massage Your Business with Purpose, Passion and Perseverance*. She can be reached at charlotte@charlotteirwin.com or 586-268-5444.

If You Believe It, You Can Achieve It

By Rene Dechert and Rick Marose

You can't do that for a living.

You need to get a regular job.

Where's your job security?

Do you know how many businesses are failing?

You expect to start a business in this economy?

Expanding your business is just being greedy.

A rich man can't get into heaven.

You're not educated enough to teach your kids.

Why would anyone want to go there?

Do any of these sound familiar to you? Have you heard any of these questions from your family or your friends? We've heard these and many similar other statements over the years. Often it seems that they are only trying to help you and make you see the reality of the situation. Right!? Sometimes we even start to believe them. Sometimes we start to doubt ourselves and buy into their view of the world. That only compounds the problem and sends us spiraling down into ultimate failure. It's like a cancer that consumes us until we succumb and let them drag us down into mediocrity.

Create Your Job Security

When the housing market crashed in 1979 my then husband, a finish carpenter, and I decided to make and sell wooden toys, mirrors, clothe dolls, and stuffed animals at craft shows to earn some money. With marginal success at that we decided to try something new to Michigan - a renaissance festival. We brain stormed some ideas and decided to make some wooden swords and shields. Before the first event was over we knew it would be a viable source of income. We applied to other shows that we began to hear about around the country. We knew that this was where we belonged. We withstood a great deal of criticism from family and friends alike. "Do you think your Dad enjoyed what he did? No. But he did it anyway to support the family," my mother said to me. "Your husband should find a job with security." "How do you expect to make a living at this?" Some of my family still has problems with our lifestyle though most of them have given up trying to change us. Despite what they thought we persisted in our belief about the business and it now extends from Arizona to Maryland and from Connecticut to Florida. My present husband and I even took the business into Canada 12 years ago. We have also set up three of our five sons in their own shows to start them off with their own businesses. Had we given in to what others said who knows what we would be doing today! Job security comes from within not without.

Educate Yourself

With this change in our lifestyle home schooling seemed like the logical thing to do. It was not as well accepted back 20 years ago and so we were beset again with criticism from family and friends. "What about their social life?" "You don't have enough education to teach your kids." It took a lot of belief in myself to realize that with a little help from friends I could give my kids a more well rounded education with better field trips than they could ever get in regular school. I believe they have not suffered from lack of formal education and got better social interaction from traveling than they could ever have gotten in school. We have taught them self reliance and to have a belief in themselves to do whatever they put their minds to. We learned a lot ourselves and realized that schooling is more about learning how to learn not so much about learning all the names, dates, places, etc.

Trust Your Instincts

Several years after my first husband and I started the business, I knew the only way I, Rene, could survive as an individual was to leave him and split the business with him. I knew I was more than just his wife and the mother of his kids. I had dreams of my own that he was unwilling to accept. Again I was met with criticism from family and friends alike. "Just stay with it." "Stay with him for the kids' sake." "What makes you think it will be any easier on your own?" He even said,"You're taking the easy way out." But it wasn't the easy way out for me. I still loved him but I had to love myself more and knew divorce was the right thing for me and was the only way Rene could survive. It was my heartfelt belief in myself - that I could make it alone- that allowed me to do what I needed to do.

Be Persistent

During the time of my divorce I began suffering from lower back pain. I went to my doctor and he couldn't help. Then I went to an acupuncturist and he told me I would have to live with the pain as there was nothing else he could do for me. Believing there had to be another solution I began researching alternatives. I was introduced to a book called "You Can Heal Your Life". The author's philosophy is that most illness comes from within and not from without. Lower back pain can be an indication of fear of the future and lack of financial support. Here I was in the midst of a divorce. Can you say fear of the future and lack of financial support! That realization got rid of most of the lower back pain. Amazing what a little education can do for your belief system!

My journey taught me early on that I needed to believe in myself and not listen to what others said. It wasn't always easy but I found that if I persisted in what I believed in I could accomplish anything. It has been a life long educational process that still goes on today. I am continually being the best I can be by reading inspirational and self empowerment books, going to seminars, learning more about…

Throughout the years we learned a lot and found the following quite helpful:

Step One: Define your dream.

Ask yourself what are you passionate about? What makes you happy? What do your instincts tell you? Is this really what you want to do or is it something someone else wants you to do? Only you can answer these questions. You have to do what's right for you.

Step Two: Set your goal.

When I married my second husband, Rick, we both knew we wanted to have a bed and breakfast. When the house we now own came up for sale again after I had looked at it 4 years previous and at $25,000 less than had been previously listed I knew this was the place we were meant to create our bed and breakfast. That was our main objective and although we had gotten sidetracked with home schooling 3 of our boys, our sword business and life itself - the vision and the goal remained and grew stronger and larger.

Step Three: Keep positive and educate yourself.

Read and listen to inspirational and informational CD's that keep you inspired and informed about your business. Throughout the ensuing years we found authors like Louise Hay, Wayne Dyer, Deepak Chopra, and James Ray to keep us inspired and on the right track. We also began reading books on the bed and breakfast industry so we would have a better idea of what we would encounter along the way. We learned about associations to join and the advantages of belonging to them. We began to form relationships to build the team we would need. We found there is a lot of help for you out there and all you have to do is tap into it. We also learned the dance of local governments and what they would require of us. Every step brought us closer and closer to our objective.

Step Four: Create a vision board.

One of the things that keeps me excited is creating a vision board. I know you probably think this is a little silly, but as you see more and more of the details and fill them in on the board, the stronger and clearer the vision becomes. I tape a $100 bill to my board to remind myself of success and prosperity. Our bed and breakfast has grown from a simple

B&B into a country manor with an organic tearoom with fantasy cottages to let.

Step Five: Create a plan.

You need not create all the details of how you are going to get there. See the destination and don't worry about each turn in the road. There may be a few detours but know you're on the right path. There will be challenges but keep the final destination firmly in your mind and know that in the end it will all be worth the journey.

Never Stop Dreaming

The next chapter in our life is no less scary. We are creating The Entwood Manor and Peacock Tearoom. It will have a 40 seat organic restaurant and three suites to rent as well as several fantasy cottages to let. This is situated on nearly 8 acres (including a 2 acre pond) in the northwest corner of Oakland County, Michigan, conveniently located adjacent to the renaissance festival that began our other business. "But why there?" "Who would want to go there?" We had a vision when we bought this house 16 years ago that we would have a bed and breakfast. That vision may have taken a long time to come to fruition but our belief in that vision has not faded but rather grown as we believe more and more that we can achieve anything we put our minds to. Entwood Manor is a destination. What next!

About the Authors:

Rick Marose and Rene Dechert are dreamers who wish to follow their hearts instead of what is conventional. They are entrepreneurs who have taught their children to be successful entrepreneurs as well. They are available to inspire you and your group with stories of their exciting adventures. They can be reached at 248-634-3165 or at swan@tir.com.

The Joys and Sorrows of a Serial Entrepreneur
By Latif Muhaimeen

My family moved to the United States from Bangladesh in December 1975. I was just 11 years old and very excited about the prospects of living in America.

Gas Station Attendant:

I remember my father's amazing work ethic as a gas station manager. He later bought the gas station in Benton Harbor, MI, in 1976. Because he was a successful businessman and an engineer in Bangladesh, he found ways to make the establishment profitable. I spent a lot of time there learning the value of hard work and good service.

Growing up, I worked many part-time jobs; as a waiter, babysitter, landscaper, paperboy, assembly line worker, cook, to selling knives and artwork from the trunk of my car. My parents pushed me to become a physician or an engineer, instead I rebelled and dropped out of college and went backpacking thru Europe. Though my mother is a psychiatrist, and my father a civil engineer, I always wanted to become a businessman. I was not sure exactly how to get started.

Profitable Bookmaker:

As a student at University of Detroit, I thought a bookmaking operation would be a good way to make money. I was the campus bookie and I made more money in one football season than most college graduates did in a year! My college dean admitted that my activity was creative, but it had absolutely no place in college. He encouraged me to use my business skills positively to benefit myself and the communities around me. This was a lesson well learned.

A transition job to pay for college:

I always looked up to millionaire entrepreneurs and real estate moguls like Rockefeller and Trump. I was awed by their success. I picked up a real estate license while completing my MBA at the University of Detroit. At the time, real estate was just part time because I was also working at Meijer as a manager making only $18,000 a year.

I started working in the paint and plumbing department and soon got promoted to managing the store maintenance crew. At that time, Meijer had a tuition assistance program, which helped with my MBA.

Real Estate Agent and Investor:

As a full time real estate agent with Century 21 in West Bloomfield, I was finally in charge of my future. I worked under a very successful broker, Ron Berman, who was the first to teach me about real estate.

Later I joined Hannett, Wilson and Whitehouse in Birmingham. Kathy Wilson, the broker, recruited me there and was my mentor. She was incredibly successful and had an amazing ability to connect with all her clients on a personal level. My goal in real estate was to own 100 rental properties before the age of 30. Although I didn't achieve my goal, I was close, owning 86 units at one point in my career. My math was quite simple. If I had a net cash flow of $200 per unit per month, it would generate a yearly cash flow of $240,000 plus appreciation! My portfolio kept growing in the 90s till we hit the worst real estate market in 2006. I had to reorganize my portfolio and re-strategize. When people ask me why I chose to be a realtor, I tell them that Real Estate is my passion, I love what I do. I have no ceiling on my earnings. I still recall the excitement I felt when I received a $96,000 commission check on a $2.4 million deal!

100 business cards and 12 clients and a referral from my 4 year old:

When I moved to my new house in Bloomfield in 1996, I was looking for a person to maintain my lawn and I was referred to Yusuf. He was an engineer from Bosnia and was also a soldier. Following an injury in the Bosnian war he moved to the US. He worked 7 days a week, 12 hours each day. Yusuf cut the grass of many successful doctors, lawyers and business professionals in the area.

We made a deal that had an amazing impact on my business. Once over dinner, I gave him 100 business cards and asked him to pass them to his clients. In return, I would promote him to 100 of my clients. He referred me 21 clients and I closed 12 transactions with an average home value of $380,000.

From my experience with Yusuf, I learned the importance of taking advantage of available opportunities and asking for referrals. One single person can elevate your business.

I even got a referral from my 4 year old daughter, Emma. She always tells people, "My poppa is a 'realestater', can he sell you a house?" One of her classmate's mother asked me to list her house because she heard so much great things about me from Emma!

What would success be without failure?

In 2003, I invested $150,000 in a restaurant named 'Masala Bistro' in Troy. Though the food was excellent and the critics ranted and raved, my venture was an utter failure. I had no business model. I overpaid my staff, paid premiums for supplies, had untrained management and lacked a contingency plan. I eventually had to close it down.

From this venture, I learned:
1. Importance of an operating business plan.
2. Consult industry professionals, prior to investing.
3. Stick to what you know best.
4. Without successful management, business will eventually fail.

How to succeed in today's market:

This is a tough real estate market—property values have plummeted, and people are losing their jobs and homes to foreclosure. The most important thing is to stay positive, adapt to the environment and change your marketing plan. For example, I am contacting the loss mitigation departments at banks to let them know they could rely on my services. I am calling on sellers who are falling behind on mortgage.

To separate myself from other realtors, this is what I offer them:
A) Professional, educated and with over 15 years real estate experience
B) Well versed in the field of short sale and foreclosure
C) Able to connect with the sellers' situation
D) Expert negotiator who will get the best price for their home
E) Excellent market knowledge and will be able to price the property properly
E) Excellent follow up, so they will know exactly what is going on at all times
F) I am a closer. I will be able to CLOSE the deal and will maintain close communication between all parties throughout the process.

I was fortunate to receive tremendous amount of business from banks and sellers in distress. Even during the downturn in the economy, I was able to reposition myself and had one of my best years in one of the worst real estate market.

I believe in certain core competencies that have to be satisfied to achieve success in the business realm. They are:
1. Possess working knowledge about the product and the industry.
2. Adapt to the current market.
3. Capitalize on available marketing opportunities.
4. Prioritize the client's best interest.
5. Connect with your client base.
6. Exceed your clients' expectations: A signed thank you letter can do wonders.
7. Follow thru with your promises.

Entrepreneurship has given me opportunities to travel the world and also enjoy friendships with very successful and inspiring individuals.

Here are some experiences which have had a lasting impact in my life.

Story of majhee- the fisherman

Traveling is my true passion and I have visited over 45 countries. A few years ago, I visited Bangladesh to learn about my parents' country. I always immerse myself into the culture and get a glimpse of the everyday life of ordinary people. I hired Karim, a majhee (fisherman), to be my guide. We took an amazing 4-night journey on his little canoe and went from one village to another. He lived with his wife and two young daughters in a one room mud hut which didn't have running water or electricity. He grew vegetables in his yard and sold them along with his daily catch at the local bazaar. His average monthly income was only $20 US. Karim had a beautiful smile; cheerful and optimistic all the time.

One night, I asked Karim, "What is the secret of your happiness?" He looked at me in surprise and said, "I wake up every morning and see the smile on my daughter's face. The beautiful sun is shining on my glorious garden. My family is healthy. I have my lucky fishing net, fertile soil to farm, food for my family, and a roof over my head. I'm so much better off than so many others. What more could I want?"

Karim taught me the true meaning of happiness. As I work through the current real estate market, I remember him.

Story of the Amazon

In 2002, I had an incredible experience of spending a week in the depths of the Amazon jungle in Brazil. I spent a week in a tree house deep in the rain forest. Spending a few days with the indigenous people made me appreciate what I had back in America. Their lives were very simple. They were hunters and gatherers and wore clothes made from leaves and leather.

Everything they needed for their survival was found in the Amazon. They were all happy, caring and extremely loving. They gave me several handicrafts, which I display in my office. From this tribe, I learned that happiness is derived from one's heart, not material possessions. We must use all available tools to our business a total success.

Two very inspiring clients that I have had the fortune of working with are Albert Scaglione and Dr. Mehul Mehta.

Albert Scaglione, the CEO of Park West Gallery, is one of my favorite clients and a true American success. He owns Park West Gallery the world's largest private art dealer. It has over 1.2 million clients, and maintains a 63,000 sq.ft. gallery in Southfield, Michigan and a 181,000 sq.ft. facility in Miami. I admire his achievements and I am proud to be his realtor for the past 15 years. I have implemented many of his ideas in my business.

Dr Mehul Mehta is one of the most successful hand surgeons in Michigan. He also belongs to a group of medical doctors who annually visit a third world country and perform surgery for the underprivileged children in remote villages. I am proud to be his realtor and close friend.

I try to live by these words, so eloquently stated by John D. Rockefeller; "In the choice of your profession or your business employment, let your first thought be: Where can I lend a hand in a way most effective to advance the general interests? Enter life in such a sprit, choose your vocation in that way, and you have taken the first step on the highest road to a large success."

I want to end this simple story with one key idea. Being a business owner has its trials and tribulations but the joy of being in charge of one's own destiny trumps them all.

I wish you a fun-filled and prosperous journey as well.

"Latif's patience, business-savvy and professionalism have se-cured his place as our lifetime realtor. We never hesitate to refer him to anyone in need of an agent. He's simply the best!"
— THERESA ANDARE M.A. L.L.P., Psychotherapist and Business Owner, Bloomfield Hills, MI

"Latif has been my realtor and a friend for the past 15 years. His loyalty, dedication, knowledge and understanding of the housing market is truly remarkable. He is the best of the best. Latif is trustworthy, honest and my realtor for life!"
— MARC SCAGLIONE, President, Park West Gallery, Southfield, MI

About The Author:

Latif Muhaimeen is a top real estate agent with Max Brook Realtors in Birmingham. He has been a resident of Birmingham/Bloomfield Hills community for over 30 years and sold more than $200,000,000 in Real Estate. He is ranked among the top 1% of realtors nationwide.

Latif can be contacted at latif@muhaimeen.com or (248) 760-1208. Website: www.LatifRealtor.com

As a promotion, Latif will give a $100 gift card to anyone who refers a client who closes.

How To Design Your Future
NLP Strategies That Work
By Anna Russo

Are you feeling challenged in today's global marketplace? Would you like to become more certain about how to achieve your goals and dreams?

The first impulse is to get more information about the market, your clients and learn the tools to compete *but the reality is that what you need first is to master your communication with yourself and others.*

Wow! Imagine having a manual for you, the reader, that you can utilize with your friends, family, at work and in business - anybody you interact with on a daily basis! Building successful relationships in the 21st century is a must! Let us help you get an inside track on achieving this goal.

When you use the strategies recommended here not only will you become a better business owner/manager, but you will also be a more balanced person. These strategies will assist you in finding your strengths and motivation to stay focused on your outcome regardless of the economic conditions; resulting in more satisfaction and fulfillment in life.

In my 30+ years as business owner, Certified Life Coach, Neuro-Linguistic Programming Trainer, and author, I have utilized these strategies in understanding human behavior and helping individuals and companies, make the impossible become possible, and the possible easier.

Why is succeeding becoming more challenging than ever before?

Five reasons for the challenges are:
1. Global Market
2. People are asking more questions
3. More information is available
4. Increased competition
5. Abundance has made people more selective

So how do you overcome these challenges and become successful?

People that are successful in business are providing answers and fulfilling people's needs. They know how to build rapport with others and they have a commitment to provide the best quality service.

People who succeed have specific formulae. They know what they want and they proceed step by step until they get their outcome. They are committed and don't get discouraged by difficulties or set-backs.

<u>Guaranteed Formula for Success:</u>
1. Focus on the outcome.
2. Gain and maintain rapport.
3. Be flexible (easily adjusting to new situations).
4. Know how to ask questions to gain clarity about what people want.

1. Focus on the Outcome

I find that many people are focused on avoiding problems or failing. Their communication sounds this way: "I don't want to fail", or, "I don't want a problem". More than likely you just made that image in your mind, didn't you? The brain does not understand "don't". For the brain to make meaning of words it must visualize the word. Do you realize the importance of being focused on the outcome and speak in terms of the outcome, "I want to succeed or I am looking for a solution".

The other side of failure is success, and the other side of a problem is a solution! I have worked with hundreds of thousands of individuals and business owners who have been surprised with this distinction: **failure or success; problem or solution**. Those who have decided on success or a solution have doubled their income and improved their results in a short period of time. What you choose is entirely up to you.

Are you clear on the outcome you desire?

Ask yourself, "Is this a commitment or just a good idea"? If it is a

commitment, follow these guidelines:
- Lay the groundwork. Be clear about what you want and what has prevented you from getting it in the past.
- Interrupt the pattern of belief that is preventing you from moving forward.
- When you look at the outcome, do you see a clear picture?
- Is your self-talk inviting you towards your outcome? If it isn't, adjust your tone of voice. Make it encouraging. It will change your feelings and attitude towards yourself and outcome.

2. *Gaining and Maintaining Rapport*

Clients trust and do business with those individuals that they are comfortable with. Your focus needs to be on establishing instant rapport with the client. There are several components to rapport. Each individual has a different model of the world. That means they may interpret things differently according to how they look at a situation. As you build rapport, you connect and have a better chance to influence your clients in a positive way, because they are paying attention to your message. The way you build rapport is by matching their language, gesture, posture/ body language, tone of voice and style of communication.

The next time you are interacting with someone, I invite you to pay attention to their communication style. You will be surprised at what you will discover. As human beings, we use the five senses to communicate.

The five senses are: sight, sound, touch, smell and taste.

Most of us prefer using one sense and use it consistently without realizing

if we are matching the people we speak to. To have a balance in life and be able to reach more people, we need to practice using all the senses.

1. **Sight** – People who interpret the world visually make pictures of what you are saying. They also speak very fast and use visual words, i.e. "Can you <u>see</u> what I am saying?"
2. **Sound** – These individuals interpret the world through sounds.

They pay attention to words and sounds. They say, i.e., "I heard what you said". You will notice that their tone of voice is more monotonous compared to others.

3. **Emotions/Touch** – Those who interpret their experiences through their feelings based on how they feel may say, "I need to sleep on it", or, "this doesn't feel good". These people pay attention to how they feel when you are communicating with them.

4. **Taste/Smell go together and are often connected with feelings.** Here are a few comments you may have heard: "I can almost taste it," or, "the sweet smell of success." Someone who might make these statements is already feeling good about themselves.

When it comes to building relationships with people, if you don't pay attention to the importance of their communication style, it is like speaking another language and rapport is hard to establish.

This may not be part of your routine and you may think that this takes a lot of work. However, you do not need to change your identity to integrate these new skills. Because we are creatures of habit, this will require practice and a new mind-set. There are many things that you do every day, like breathing, and you don't even have to think about it. After you practice these new skills, they become just as automatic as breathing. You can do it!

If you are really committed to being successful, why not implement these techniques, and shorten the amount of time it takes to create and build relationships! You already know the results you got from your old style-sometimes you were successful, and sometimes you weren't. Neuro Linguistic Programming is proven to work. When you use these strategies you get consistently positive results. Why not make this a part of your routine?

3. *Be Flexible*

Have you heard people complain – things are not working for them, life is hard, this isn't fair, and other people don't understand them?

Successful people quickly adapt to a variety of situations and people.

Successful individuals do not get discouraged. They have the attitude that difficulties present opportunities to practice their skills and knowledge.

Flexible individuals are more focused on their surroundings (external). They know what their outcome is. People like that stay on track! Such people change their approach according to what the situation requires.

How would you answer these questions?
Am I flexible?
Am I committed to being successful?
What is stopping me?
What skills do I have?
What additional skills do I need?
Am I willing to do what it takes to get the success I want?

4. *How to Ask the Right Questions*

Do you remember the last time you walked away from an exchange wishing you had said 'this or that' to the other person? Do you know what happened? It seems like your mind went blank. You knew the answer was somewhere in your mind but you couldn't get it out. Were you uptight because the people were not agreeing with you? Were you focusing too much on making the sale and not hearing the conversation? Did you miss the need of your client?

Consider this example: A successful printing and copy shop owner had been in business for awhile but found the current economy discouraging. He had business expenses including vacant office space, a home, children in college and other personal obligations. He was becoming very concerned about meeting expenses and started to have negative self-talk like, "Oh no, I am going to lose everything. Times are so hard and nobody is listening. Why should I even get up in the morning?" You can imagine how his affected his attitude, not to mention how he slipped into a depression as a result.

- When I met with this individual, I started out using open-ended questions like:
- What can you do to promote yourself?
- What would you not do to change? (negative self-talk)
- What are you willing to do?
- What can you be grateful for? (used to create a shift in perspective and emotions)
- Who do you know that needs your products?
- Do you know people that are happy and motivated even in tough times, and are doing well?
- What are they doing different than you that attracts business?

By asking yourself these questions, you can change how you feel about yourself. Your approach to clients changes because you are now in a positive frame of mind ready to take action.

When we ask the right questions, it is hard avoiding an answer!

Ask clear, open-ended questions that allow the people to see themselves motivated, what they want and what kind of actions to take.

When people communicate throughout their presentation they are revealing what is important to them. Are you listening and hearing what is important to them? What would take care of their needs? Many people are eager to get a contract and don't pay attention to rapport.

Your clients want to know how your product will benefit them.

How do you go about asking the questions to know what they need?

1. Start your conversation with small talk.
2. Learn a little bit about them (people love to talk about themselves).
3. Keep them engaged with questions and watch their body language.
4. Securing the appointment. When you find it difficult to get an appointment with a client, try this approach:

Client: "I am too busy to meet with you."
Response: "I am happy to hear that you are busy.
I specialized in helping people like you who are
very busy. I help them improve their business
in a short period of time. Are you interested in
making more money while you have more time to
enjoy life?"
Client: "Yes, I might be interested".
Response: "When would be better for you?
Offer a couple of different time to make sure they don't slam
the door shut.

5. Keep focused on your desired outcome. Once you and the
client get together, discuss what he/she wants to accomplish
in thirty days, one year, and five years. The answer will lead
you to present how you can help the client get there easier and
faster than the competition. By using your product or service,
they will have reliability, commitment and quality because
those are the things you provide.

Communication is all about what the other person hears. Use a
tone of voice that allows the clients to imagine what you are talking
about. Practice this and watch your business skyrocket. Help your
client succeed and you become even more successful.

Can you apply this in your personal life?

The outcome will be: turning your business around in a short
period of time, making more money; finding balance in your life;
creating better relationships, having better health, and happiness will
be your outcome.

Commit to Grow

This is what we call designing your life.

"Anna Russo is one of the most knowledgeable NLP Trainers and Life Coaches I have come across. I trust her professionally as well as personally. I am impressed with the way she helps people create changes quickly and easily. I recommend her training to anybody that wants to live at their full potential."
—MIKE BRIDGES, G.M. / ABB, Inc., Auburn Hills, MI

About the Author:

Anna Russo, author of <u>Connecting With Resistant Teenagers, Ten Proven Steps</u>, is one of the top Certified Trainers in the field of Neuro-Linguistic Programming (NLP), Author, Certified Life Coach and Speaker.

Russo designs and implements Communication Programs for Business to enhance: Relationships, Sales, Rapport and Management and Personal Development. She coaches individuals and business to design the future they want.

Ms. Russo has offices in Troy and Grosse Pointe, MI. She can be contacted at:

248.528.0753
successstrategiesnlp.com
annaru@comcast.net

Brain Fitness – The Secret To Peak Mental Performance

By Jane Stewart Ph.D.

There is a simple way to make your life easier and more productive! In this chapter you can learn the four steps to improve your mental performance to enjoy more benefits from your work effort.

The February 2008 issue of Newsweek reports that scientists have found several factors that go hand in hand with better mental performance. These factors include education, professional success, as well as intellectual, social, and physical activities. Dr. Joseph Sanford originator of the **Braintrain** cognitive training software says twenty hours on his **Captain's Log** cognitive training program can improve a person's attention score. One person's score went from 80 to 130.

Staying mentally fit is a life long process. People all learn differently. At one time I found it challenging to stay focused and perform at my best over long periods of time. Fortunately I discovered actions to help me improve and ways to do things which now work for me with consistent success.

I am a Michigan Certified Teacher with a Special Education endorsement in Emotionally Impaired. My masters and doctoral work are in special education. Experts diagnosed me as being ADHD and dyslexic. My own journey led me to start my tutoring business in 1992. I have been assisting children and adults to overcome the challenges which I have battled with all my life. I have lived and taught in Illinois, Indiana, as well as Michigan. Some of my business experience can be traced to owning and running a restaurant and party store as well. Today I frequently consult with schools and speak to groups of teachers and parents to help them and their students and children. Brain based learning is a new hot topic in education, adapting instruction to learning styles makes sense.

My problems started when I was a student. The teaching style in school made it difficult for me to learn. Some of my bosses supervised me in ways which were incompatible to my mental strengths and weaknesses. I was immensely frustrated and stressed everyday. After intense research and willingness to work through my problems, I found ways to achieve success, and now I share my success techniques professionally to help others who might be experiencing the same frustrations.

Let's go over the four steps to creating unbelievable results by improving brain fitness.

1. **Recognize that you have a problem and make a decision to do something about it.** Please take a moment and answer the following queries as honestly as possible:

- Are you worried about losing your job?
- Are other people getting raises and promotions while you are not?
- Does your boss question your capabilities?
- Do you have too much work and not enough time?
- Are you becoming forgetful?
- Are you too tired at the end of the work day to do anything else?
- Do you lose your temper easily and become angry?
- Do other people annoy you a lot?
- Do you have trouble sleeping?
- Is stress and anxiety a part of your life?
- Are you feeling incompetent?
- Are you having relationship problems?
- Do you have trouble finishing things you start?
- Are you still confused about what is a good job for you?

In the past I answered yes to all of these questions, so if you found yourself in a similar boat; I fully understand. I found solutions and you can too.

As the job world is changing and new skills are becoming a necessity you can find help and end up a happier person. How do I know this can happen? **I improved and now help other people find their personal roads to happiness.**

Memory, attention, processing speed, and organization are four major brain functions which are critical to one's ability to do work. Once a person has a clear picture of his/her learning strengths and weaknesses, he/she can begin to fix the problem. The brain is a muscle and responds to strengthening and conditioning just like any other muscle. It likes to be challenged. As people continue to learn new tasks and improve performance on challenging tasks, they can take their performance to new levels. Improving these brain functions also helps with slowing the aging process.

2. **The second step is to address the problem** and this step begins by having a positive mental attitude with an expectation that things can improve. At this point, you are willing to do the work necessary for the improvement to occur. Start with identifying the problem and setting clear goals. Write down a personal goal list that includes obstacles standing in your way.

Think back to when you were in school:
- Was that a fun time in your life or was it a daily nightmare?
- Did you have trouble paying attention?
- Did you have trouble listening?
- Were you disorganized?
- Was reading, writing or math a challenge?
- Did you have trouble memorizing things?
- Did you forget to turn in your work?
- Was the teacher difficult to understand?

Today, perhaps you do not have enough education, knowledge and/or skills to advance to the next performance level in your career. For example, you are a great sales representative you understand the product you are selling and have great interpersonal relationships with your clients. You love the freedom of setting your own schedule and having your administrative assistant doing your paper work. The big day comes and the company offers you "the big promotion". What can you do? If you say, "No" you create a problem, if you say; "Yes" you create bigger problems. The promotion means more money and more prestige, but it also means you might have to do mental work including taking on responsibilities which could be too challenging and could highlight your weaknesses. What do you do now? If you sincerely want the promotion, there are professionals available to help you with this step of addressing your problem.

3. **The next important step is to diagnose and understand how you learn.** The three primary channels that people use to learn and process information when they are doing mental work are visual, auditory, and

kinesthetic. Different parts of the brain control each one of these channels. If one channel is very weak and **is an important channel you need to learn, then your problem is negatively impacting your success and progress.** Different types of jobs favor different learning channels. A person tends to choose work compatible with her brain's strengths and weaknesses.

Another consideration is whether a person is left brain or right brain dominant. People who are strong left brain processors are usually good at planning, organizing, paying attention to detail, spoken language, and number skills. People who are strong right brain learners are usually good at seeing the big picture, imagination, spatial tasks, and emotionally intuitive. Writing for example requires you to integrate right and left brain tasks to get the job completed.

For example, a person who is a kinesthetic learner will want to do active work such as construction, sports, or outside sales. A person who is a strong visual learner might prefer to be an author, artist, or financial advisor. A person who is a strong auditory learner might want to be a musician, a sales person or a lawyer. Research shows different ways to think about you: multiple intelligences, and emotional intelligence. Yes these are important, but **reading comprehension remains the essential tool for mental work.**

Time management and organization are the essential qualities/ habits to successful learning and work productivity. A person can find these tasks challenging if they have poor visual attention and processing skills. Imagine if you could spend half the time reading necessary emails or read twice as many emails in the same time you are now spending! There are many courses and programs available to increase your reading speed, but what is the benefit of increased reading speed if you do not understand what you are reading? I prefer to think about **EFFECIENT READING:** reading quickly with understanding. Speed reading programs can improve speed while allowing the reader to be able to comprehend the material. Bill, a 49 year old law student, used the *EYEQ Speed Reading Program* to help. His reading speed went from 500 words per minute to 1500 wpm. His grades went from Cs to As.

When thinking about improving reading, you may need to

consider if you can understand the vocabulary, see a mental picture formed by the words, hear the words, and actually have the words come alive.

Next you have to identify the problem and set some goals.
- Do you have trouble paying attention?
- Do you have trouble listening?
- Are you disorganized?
- Is reading, writing or math a challenge?

Perhaps you do not have enough technical knowledge in the field of work you want or are asked to pursue. **Professional resources are available to help you with this step.** When I was fifty I found out I was ADHD and dyslexic. When I began addressing these issues, my life began an upward swing which continues unabated. My life keeps getting easier and more productive.

The brain is a muscle and as one ages it becomes more and more important to take care of it.

Eating brain friendly food is imperative. Proteins work on keeping the physical cells in the brain elastic and flexible. Carbohydrates are the food required for mental work. Check the diets which athletes follow. Heart smart and diabetic diets are great for the brain. The B vitamins are good brain helpers especially B-12 and Folic Acid. Antioxidants are also important. It is important to eat continually throughout the day. One trainer, Joe, tells his clients to eat breakfast like a king, lunch like a prince, and dinner like a pauper. Actually trainers, nutritionists, and doctors are recommending several small meals rich in natural fruits, veggies, and fiber. Check with your physician or nutrients to develop a healthy diet for peak mental performance.

Stress and anxiety are two huge villains when one is trying to do mental work. On a continuum: learn how to use visualization, meditation, and self hypnosis to stay relaxed so the brain can focus all of its energy on the mental work. Meditation and visualization also help with keeping a positive mental attitude. One has to believe that one can achieve before the achievement can happen.

Physical exercise is also important. Thirty minutes of activity each day helps. To do the higher level work which separates humans from other animals, one needs to take care of basic physical needs first. *Sleep* is important for commanding mental performance. If a person takes care of his/her brain, the brain will take care of them.

Now you know what kind of learner you are and what is impacting your mental performance.

4. *The next step is to find a brain coach! The Optiminds Brain Fitness Program* helps clients develop an individualized improvement plan to help achieve performance goals. Alex, a client, writes, "I am an ADHD adult, and I have worked with Jane for nearly a decade. She has directly helped shape my professional career. We started working in high school, by focusing on my learning strengths she was able to help me succeed. Now as an adult my brain has not changed, but I know how it works and how to utilize my strengths." The coach will suggest schedule changes to implement as well as exercises that strengthen and condition the brain. Technology is available to speed up this improvement process.

At the beginning one can expect to spend between thirty minutes to one hour each day five days a week. Noticeable results can be seen after just twenty hours. As time goes on, the client and the coach will tweak and modify the processes and exercises. The process should see significant progress within three months. The brain coach will then continue to help on as needed basis after the intensive intervention. .

Dr. Neil Fiore, a California psychologist gives 4 Simple Steps to overcoming hurdles and helps accomplish your goals:

1. Define your goal,

2. Commit to change,

3. Take action, and

4. Bounce-back from setbacks.

If you are experiencing any of the challenges we have discussed then get started now on the first day of **your NEW LIFE.** Brain fitness helps a person identify their cognitive strengths and weaknesses and find ways to learn more, faster, remember material better, and use the information productively. Get started on your personal brain fitness plan. You can get your free "Brain Fitness Diagnostics" at OPTIMINDS 248.496.0150 or jstewart@optimindsct.com.

"Dr. Jane Stewart puts a new spin on the way to achieve peak mental performance. Challenges don't have to stand in the way."
　　—Patricia Pearson, MA, CI, CEO Harbor Center

About the Author:

Jane Stewart Ph.D. is the founder of Optiminds which helps children and adults alike to cope with a demanding learning environment. The business is located in Southfield, MI. You can contact her at 248.496.0150 or jstewart@optimindsct.com.

Create A Simple, Single Page Business Plan

BY AMY GROSSMAN

A business page on a single page is quick to write, easy to update, and proven to be effective

Do you really need a business plan?

The answer is yes. But before we get into why you should write a business plan, let's explore a few of the thoughts that often come up as reasons not to have a plan. Maybe you've had some of these thoughts, as well.

"I'm too busy running my business."

"I've been doing okay without a plan."

"Writing a business plan seems too complicated and time consuming."

These are common thoughts. Let's take a closer look at them.

Being too busy can be a warning sign

Sometimes very busy people are spending time on the wrong things. For instance, a business owner may be well organized with a daily "To Do" list. It may even be prioritized. We've been taught that this is a good time management technique. The problem is that a "To Do" list is action oriented, but it is not necessarily strategic.

Michael Gerber author of the classic business book, **The E-Myth Revisited**, describes this trap as working *in* your business rather than *on* your business. This means that if you don't plan your actions according to a bigger picture of what you want for your business, you're more likely not to get the results you want.

A lack of planning is one of the top three reasons that businesses fail, according to the Small Business Development Center. There is truth to the old saying, "Failing to plan is planning to fail."

Any time is the right time to write a plan

Some businesses start with a written plan. Many more do not. Or they write the proverbial few sentences on a napkin. If you've been running your business without a written plan, now is the right time to put your plan in writing.

There is power to putting the business ideas on paper. Just the simple act of writing creates clarity and greater intention of purpose. By settling on some specific goals, you have a way to measure results and make course corrections.

Some of the biggest benefits of a business plan are its ability to help create focus, to encourage big picture thinking and to help in making decisions for the long-term — as well as and the short-term - in a way that consistently moves the business forward.

There's more than one way to write a business plan

If you search the Internet for an outline of the parts of a business plan, you'll find what I call the "classic outline." It hasn't changed in 30 years, even though the business world has changed dramatically in that time. The "classic plan" was created before the Internet existed and the boom in home-based businesses. In my opinion, the "classic outline" deters many people from writing a plan. It's long and complicated. It is not action-oriented. It assumes there will be a management team. It assumes the business is aiming to claim a significant share of a market. It assumes there will be outside financing. For many small businesses, some or all of these assumptions are not valid. I've seen many people begin to write a plan, but get discouraged or overwhelmed and never finish it. Or they have written a 30+ page plan and then find it is too theoretical to be useful. There is a shorter, more actionable plan for you to consider.

A One Page Business Plan® is a simple solution for including just the information you need and no more. This cuts the writing time dramatically.

More importantly, forcing yourself to discover and summarize the important information on one page encourages you to become laser focused on what is most important to the management and growth of your business.

Finding the motivation to write a plan

Peter had a problem. He opened a beauty spa two years ago and his business results have been unpredictable. He is a gifted hair stylist and loves his work. His clients are devoted to him, as well. His business drifted, though, because Peter spent little time on being strategic. His business had not flourished as he had hoped, because he focused on being a top-notch stylist at the expense of being the leader of his businesses. Then another salon in town closed its doors and its four stylists joined Peter's salon. It's at this point that Peter realized he needed to have a written plan to make the most of this opportunity.

Peter was noticing symptoms that are common to many small business owners:
- He was spending time on details that did not leverage his time
- He was feeling frustrated and tended to procrastinate
- He let day-to-day events drive his business because he lacked a strategic overview

The motivation to write a business plan can stem from a problem or an opportunity. Peter became motivated to write a plan when he realized he could significantly grow his business, but he needed a roadmap.

The next step was easy

Peter was able to write his plan in a matter of hours, not the months that a "classic plan" can take. That's because he was able to use "fill in the blank" statements to write his plan. I worked with him to do a gap analysis, SWOT analysis and visioning. We looked at past performance and set performance goals that he could track easily. When Peter's plan was completed, he had the five parts captured on a single page.

The Five Parts of a One Page Business Plan®
Vision
Mission
Objectives
Strategies
Actions

Vision

Defining your vision answers the questions of WHO you will serve and WHAT you will offer. WHO - get specific about the people who need, want and will pay for your services and products. You're finding a need and filling it. WHAT - be clear about what those services and products are. Envision your success and take the leap to "guesstimate" your revenue for the coming year, next year, and in 3 years. Create a bold vision for your business that energizes you.

Mission

Defining your mission is about how you differentiate yourself. What makes you, your services or products unique? With the recent explosion of Internet and other home-based businesses this should be your top concern - to set yourself apart from the pack.

Your mission is where your great business ideas come together with your unique characteristics, skills, experience and passion. There is one thing in your business that no one else can duplicate – YOU!

Objectives

Road races have a set distance so runners know when they have crossed the finish line. Think of finish lines for your business, as well. It's hard to know where you are headed if you don't measure your progress. Ask yourself if you measure key performance indicators to stay on track or make corrections. If you don't, pick several important measurements and track them consistently. Measure what matters and watch your performance improve immensely. This will also increase your sense of satisfaction.

Strategies

Following a daily "To Do" list is not enough to build a sustainable business. Without long-term strategies, it's easy to fall into the trap of reacting to situations rather than creating what you want. Being strategic means working on your business using systems, principles, policies and values that authentically reflect your business vision and mission.

Actions

Decide on actions that support your business vision, mission, objectives and strategies. It's hard enough to juggle all the activities of running a business. An action plan recognizes all the functions, sorts out what to do and what to delegate. Take time to write down the most important work to be done, the person responsible for doing it and by when.

The benefits are both rational and emotional

The rational benefits of having a short, highly actionable business plan are most likely easy to imagine. The emotional benefits are equally important.

- A clear, focused vision of what your business will accomplish can increase your satisfaction and fulfillment
- A compelling and consistent way to describe your business can build your confidence
- A realistic measure of current results, as well as a way of tracking improvement, can sharpen your concentration, reinforce honesty and increase a sense of accomplishment
- A written roadmap enables you to be strategic and relaxed instead of reactive and stressed out, bringing structure, freedom and consistency.
- A unified plan of action saves time and effort, bringing results, positive habits and peace of mind.

Like an elegant mathematical formula, the One Plan Business Plan® takes what was once a complicated process and makes it simple.

> *"Everything should be made as simple as possible, but not simpler."*
>
> —ALBERT EINSTEIN

About the Author:

Amy Grossman, MBA, is a One Page Business Plan® Certified Consultant who makes it easy for small business owners to write a business plan. Sign up for a FREE e-course to learn 5 keys to a highly effective plan at www.businessplanactiongroup.com.

Don't Be an Average Joe Business Owner: Start with the End in Mind

BY MARISA PETRELLA, ATTORNEY AT LAW

Last week I received an irate call from Joe, a small business owner. His business partner Randy, who was never active in their business, got a divorce and gave his ex-wife his ownership interest in the corporation. "Can you believe Randy called me to say that now I have to deal with his ex-wife?!" sputtered Joe. "She knows nothing about the business and I don't want to do business with her!"

Hire a good lawyer to avoid problems

Most business owners don't want to visit a lawyer. Joe was blunt, "I would rather get a tooth drilled than see an attorney. I was referred to you because things went wrong and you can fix it." Joe wouldn't need my help to fix the situation if he planned ahead. Business owners sometimes delay seeing an attorney when they start their business because they mistakenly suspect that the lawyer's advice may unnecessarily slow down their forward progress. They also fear the dreaded attorney fee. Locating an attorney who is business savvy, "real" and accessible is key to overcoming such misgivings. The right attorney adds value to any business operation.

Put a business plan and advisory team in place

Entrepreneurs often exude enthusiasm and nervous energy when they start a new business. They want to act fast and most neglect to prepare a comprehensive business plan. They want to meet the business's immediate needs, find suppliers, secure financing and make their business name known in the market. When I asked Joe how he started his business, he said "I just told my CPA to get a tax ID number so I could get to work!" **WHOA!** If you are starting a business, don't be an average Joe! Be an extraordinary business owner — **start with the end in mind**

— and get legal, accounting, financial and insurance advice to implement a plan that will allow you to achieve success!

Start with the end in mind

What does "start with the end in mind" mean? It means you must picture what the business will look like and how it will operate. You must also focus on your exit strategy. Yes, think exit strategy from the beginning. By focusing on the end game, you will find that it is much easier to decide on the foundation you need to put in place. Just as a good builder would not start work on a building before the foundation was complete, you should not start building a company without a business plan that includes an exit strategy.

As a small business owner, you should consider eight basic questions to help focus on achieving long-term success:

What do you need to do to protect your "big idea"?

What steps do you take to avoid personal risk?

How will you distinguish between owning and operating?

How do you choose the best business structure?

How do you acquire financial stability?

How do you reach out to the world?

Do you set a target time for length of business operation?

How do you plan a sweet ending for your exit from the company?

Answering each of these questions involves thinking beyond the immediate, and imagining what the future may hold, which helps in structuring your business. (Answering the questions is also an excellent exercise for an established business.)

PROTECT YOUR BIG IDEA

A business usually starts with an idea for a product or service that you can provide. Rather than plunge into providing this business or service, start with the end in mind and protect your interests.

What distinguishes your idea from that of others? What gives you the competitive edge? If you have developed a new product or idea, that may involve a patent (technology), or trademark (brand), or copyright (content). Even before the business begins, you want to take steps to protect your intellectual property[1].

If you do not protect your ideas, you may have a competitor "steal" that idea. Worse yet, you may have an employee "borrow" the idea when they leave your employ[2]. Or you may find that what you thought was an original idea, was already protected by someone else! If you step on someone else's rights, you may receive a "cease and desist" letter that may threaten to put you out of business.

AVOID PERSONAL RISK

One factor to consider is the liability risk of your proposed business activity. For example, a fairly simple business, like baking and selling cookies[3], may encounter significant liability if a consumer has an allergic reaction to an ingredient. While sole proprietorships and partnerships are the most simple business structures, they do not protect owners from personal liability. The consumer may sue the business **and the owner personally**, for damages suffered.

When they stop and think about it, most business owners want to avoid personal liability for actions undertaken in the ordinary course of their business. Certain business structures, like a corporation[4] or limited liability company[5] (LLC), allow the owner to be shielded from personal liability[6]. If something goes wrong, and a lawsuit results, only the assets of the business are at stake, not the assets of the owner[7].

---

1 For these questions, consult with a U.S. Patent and Trademark qualified attorney who may apply for patents, trademarks, and service marks on behalf of clients. Patent attorneys also deal with issues of patent or trademark validity, infringement, and related litigation cases.

2 A confidentiality agreement or non-compete agreement may be required of employees.

3 An entrepreneur also needs to be familiar and comply with any and all applicable governmental requirements (i.e. zoning, licensing, FDA, labeling, customs, tariff).

4 In the State of Michigan, corporations are governed by the Michigan Business Corporation Act, MCL 450.1101 - 450.2099. The governing law for your corporation is dependent upon where your Articles of Incorporation are filed.

5 In the State of Michigan, limited liability companies are governed by the Michigan Limited Liability Company Act, MCL 450.4101 - 450.5200. The governing law for your limited liability company is dependent upon where your Articles of Organization are filed, or upon the terms of the Operating Agreement.

6 Even if the owners are shielded from liability, a lawsuit may be devastating to a business. Liability insurance is a business necessity, as is having a good insurance advisor.

7 A note of caution -- the shield from personal liability is lost if an owner does not treat his company affairs separate and apart from his personal affairs.

DISTINGUISH BETWEEN OWNING AND OPERATING

In the opening scenario, Joe and Randy each owned 50% of their corporation. They both made the same financial contribution at the start of the business, but only Joe provided the know-how to run the business. Randy had been a "silent" partner, until his divorce changed the partner situation.

If Joe had consulted with an attorney when the corporation was formed, Joe would probably have been advised <u>not</u> to share ownership equally with Randy because one 50% owner can effectively block the other 50% owner from running the business. Joe had poured his time and energy into building the company and his business partner should not impede his success. A deadlock between business owners may result in costly legal battles and paralysis that end the business. Initially, most new owners do not think about ownership gridlock, because they are focused on the short-term and are in the "honeymoon" phase of their business relationship.

CHOOSE BEST BUSINESS STRUCTURE

Many small business owners begin as sole proprietors and own the business in their own names solely, or enter into a partnership with another individual. A sole proprietor requires only minimal paperwork to get started in business. In a partnership situation, the partners may draft and sign a partnership agreement, so that they may choose the terms of their relationship. If no partnership agreement is signed, or if the agreement is defective, and there is a dispute, then partnership laws in the jurisdiction where the business is located will apply[8].

Corporations are one of the most recognized forms of business structure. Corporate structure itself, because it is so familiar, facilitates business growth and expansion into national and international markets. The structure allows for separation of ownership from management, provides for change in ownership, and protects owners from personal liability.

---

8 In the State of Michigan, partnerships are governed by the Michigan Uniform Partnership Act, MCLA 449.1 – 449.2108.

Corporate structure allows for perpetual existence of the business entity. A corporation has shareholders, who own a financial interest in the company, and who may provide a source of financing the business. In addition, shareholders impact business governance; they have a say in how the business is run[9]. An owner may dream big and want his business to continue beyond his lifetime and to possibly have stock traded on a public exchange. In that case, shareholders may change on a regular basis but the corporate business continues.

A more recent addition to business structure options is a limited liability company. An Operating Agreement signed by the members (comparable to owners), allow those members to set the terms of their mutual agreement. LLCs are managed by either managers or members. The LLC business structure provides great flexibility and creativity. For example, the Operating Agreement may allow the owners to sell their membership interests in the future so that an exit strategy is in place from the beginning.

The LLC structure also compares favorably with regard to tax treatment[10]. A "C" corporation first pays income tax on its earnings at its own corporate rate and then, when those earnings are distributed to shareholders as dividends, shareholders must pay income tax on the same money again at the shareholders' own rate. Two business entities, an "S" corporation and an LLC, were created to allow the business' earnings to pass through to the owner and only be taxed once at the individual level.

ACQUIRE FINANCIAL STABILITY

How to obtain financing is an important question for business owners. Money to run the business may come from the owners through personal loans or capital contributions. If one business owner has know-how but no money, he may be better off getting a business loan through private investors, banks or the Small Business Association (SBA)[11] rather than

---

9 Corporations are managed by their directors, which are elected by the shareholders. Directors appoint officers, who must operate the day to day business of the corporation.

10 On the small business owner's team should be a Certified Public Accountant who, along with a Corporate Attorney, can provide advice regarding taxes.

11 The email address for the SBA is www.sba.gov/services/financial assistance/sbaloantopics/index.html. The SBA is a government agency charged with providing advocacy, management, procurement and financial assistance to small businesses. The SBA's Business Loan Program is one of its significant areas of financial assistance.

take on a partner only because of his cash contribution. Such outside lenders often impose requirements on the business, but will not share in the profits of the business.

An essential part of any business plan is the financial strategy for the company. Vendors and employees need to be paid and cash flow needs to be maintained, even if you are waiting for accounts receivable.

REACH OUT TO THE WORLD

Even the smallest company can do business on a global level because of the World Wide Web. An entrepreneur needs to determine where he will have his business operation, who his target market will be, and what the scope of the business will be. Many companies have a brick and mortar location, and also a presence on the internet. If you are reaching beyond your local community for customers, you should consider hiring a technology and marketing specialist for your advisory team.

SET A TARGET TIME

You may not have started the business yet, but think about how long the business will be in operation. Do you plan for it to operate until it loses profitability? Do you want to build it into a profitable enterprise and then sell it or go public?

One business owner decided to start a restaurant and to run it with his family. They knew how much time and effort that it would take to run a restaurant, so they decided to operate it for five years and then either close it, or sell it. Five years was their target time. There was no angst about what to do when they were five years into their project. They lived their dream, ran a restaurant, sold it after five years and made money in the process.

PLAN A SWEET ENDING

After all the hard work and sweat equity that goes into building a business, the entrepreneur's exit from the business should be smooth, painless and profitable. Do you plan to get residual income once you leave the business? Will you be bought out? Will the business be sold altogether?

Forward thinking owners create a business plan that projects how many and what type of employee the business will have in the future. If the employees are part of the plan, the owners must delegate certain responsibilities and create a framework for employees' compensation, benefits and separation. A prudent business owner can create interesting options for succession, which may include rewarding valued employees with an equity interest in the business. This creates business stability and allows for a smooth transition of responsibility. Most importantly, it allows the business owner to reap the benefits of his hard work at retirement.

There are also unexpected endings, which if planned for, may be made more tolerable. What happens if one of the owners of the business dies, or becomes disabled[12]? What if a co-owner divorces? What if the owners are deadlocked? Should there be restrictions on the transfer of ownership interests?

One way to anticipate these issues in a corporate structure is with a buy-sell agreement. This agreement among the business owners fixes their rights with respect to each other and provides a ready market if one of the owners wishes to sell his stock. In an LLC, the Operating Agreement provides the guidelines for such eventualities.

LAST WORD

Don't get me wrong — I am happy to represent Joe and solve his problems. But I think Joe would have been happier to pay me to help him plan in advance, rather than be threatened by litigation and a hostile business partner after years of hard work. You have the chance to avoid the same fate. Find a trusted attorney to help you start with the end in mind and build a sound business foundation to achieve business success.

---

12 *Disability and life insurance provide a financial safety net to companies, key employees, and their families in these situations.*

About the Author:

Marisa Petrella has been a Michigan lawyer for 25 years and small business owner for 12 years, which gives her a unique perspective in counseling her business clients. She provides advice regarding litigation, employee matters and employment-based immigration. Her firm is Petrella Brown PLC. and she can be reached at (248) 223-9883 or you can visit her website www.petrellabrown.com.

CHECKLIST FOR ORGANIZING A MICHIGAN BUSINESS

1. Planning Overview

    A. Review Proposed Business

        1. Type of Business to be Conducted

        2. Place or Places of Business

        3. Assets of Business

            a. Contributed by shareholders

            b. Leased?

        4. Business Plan?

    B. Owners

    C. Investment by Owners/Capital Needs

        1. Cash

        2. Property

        3. Services

        4. Bank or other financing?

        5. Securities issues in obtaining outside financing? (Exemptions—federal/state)

    D. Management Participation by Each Owner

        1. Board or Manager

        2. Officers

        3. Employees and Compensation

    E. Voting Percentages of Owners

    F. Equity Percentages (if different from voting percentages)

    G. Tax Planning

        1. Pass through entity?

2. Loans vs. equity

H. Determine whether to incorporate vs. other forms of entity

— limited liability company

— partnerships

I. Determine Whether Other Specialists are Needed — accountant

J. Licensing requirements?

K. Trademark/copyright

2. If More Than One Owner, Owner Relationships

A. Majority control

B. Minority protections

C. Minority control

D. Restrict transfers

E. Deadlock

F. Buy/sell

G. Voting Agreements

H. Documentation - shareholders and employment agreements

3. Structure

A. Choose name

B. Capital structure

Achieve Financial Freedom By Building And Selling Your Company

BY JEFF WRIGHT

As a business owner, you are working hard everyday, dealing with employee challenges, taxes, regulations and a competitive market. You must be asking - is there light at the end of the tunnel? Will I ever find the proverbial gold at the end of the rainbow?

Don't despair. I can relate. I felt the same way quite often working to build a company. Years of hard work has paid off. I was able to sell my portion of the company for a sizeable amount and I am no longer worried about my financial future.

In this chapter I wish to share some of the insights and lessons that can help you also sell your business one day and enjoy financial freedom. The road is not easy and there is some ingredient of luck required as well. Yet if you follow the steps I mention here, you too, can look forward to the day when you can cash in your chips and relax on the beach or start a new profession that excites you anew.

The Starting Point

My father is a successful entrepreneur. He owned a software company, and I learned a lot from him. David, my eventual partner, met with my current employer at the time (my father) to discuss his idea for a new software company. I was invited into the discussion as a technical consultant to give my opinion on what he should expect an outsource firm would charge to build the application for him to sell. My overriding advice was to hire a programmer to write the software and then be on board for maintenance and enhancements. And David wanted me as that guy. Let me point out that my degree was in Psychology not programming!

Even though it was risky joining a startup with my first child on the way, I took the leap since it seemed like a great opportunity and I started working with David as a partner. I designed, wrote, and maintained our software applications. As Senior VP of Development I lead the technical side of the company.

Seven Simple Steps In Building And Selling Your Company:

1. Create the best product in the marketplace

Listen to the customers and work with them to build and deliver an application that suits their needs. Building software in a bubble rarely leads to a well-received application in the field. I believed that our customers wanted a system that would make their work lives easier, not more complicated. Thus, I built everything with basic simplicity in mind. Developing fast, efficient, and durable software was the key.

Of course fulfilling a major need was a necessity as well. My partner's idea for the company was essential. So having the right product with the right target market is vitally important.

Our products were simple, easy to use, efficient, flexible, and durable. They fulfilled the prospect's needs more precisely than any other products in the market. Our goal was to "Be the best company to work with".

That entailed:
• honest and professional sales people,
• products that made the users' lives easier,
• support staff that was friendly and helpful, and
• well-trained implementers to install and train users effectively.

2. Dominate the niche by attracting vast number of users

We had the best product and were the best company in our market place. That enabled us to build an impressive number of customers. As a testament to the quality of the software application, the original version is still the number one selling product in its market nine years later. Having such a viable product and vast quantity of users made us very attractive for purchase.

3. Take the 2:30 am customer call

Here are a couple of lessons regarding customer service that could benefit you.

- From my father I learned many important lessons that were vital to my success. One such mantra was that the customer is always right. Sounds simple, but living it out is crucial to success. Customers are the livelihood of any business. If they don't feel you are on their side, they will take their business elsewhere.
- Another lesson (that was learned the hard way) was that the best customers often come from the worst implementations. Sounds strange, but it is true. When experiencing problems, you work hard with the customer to fix the situations and in the process you become a tight team and earn mutual respect and trust.
- I can remember taking a call at 2:30 in the morning and driving into work through a thunderous rain storm, just to work on a critical problem in the software that the customer needed to use first thing in the morning. I fixed the problem and the customer never forgot that dedication (even though it was our problem to fix). They became our number one reference site.
- One more lesson from my father: Do not work with the goal to make lots of money – instead, work hard while enjoying it and success will follow.
- I heard on a motivational tape early on that for every one person there are 200 people "behind" them. The thought there is that for an average wedding, the invitation list is approximately 200 people. That means that the average person has about that many personal friends, family, and business associates that they feel comfortable enough to share one of the most important days of their lives with. It also means that if they experience bad service, there is a good chance that they will share that experience with up to 200 people. That is a lot of influence.

  I needed to turn that around and say that for every great experience that I give to a prospect or customer – they may share that with 200 more. So, whether I meet a politician, mailman, teacher, young person, old person, garbage man, or executive – I treat every one of them with the respect that I would appreciate receiving myself.

4. Focus on the bottom line

People are buying a profit-making machine not a business with headaches and overhead. Run your business with an eye on the bottom line.

For the first eight years of our business we were so focused on building success that we often made decisions without respect for how it affected the bottom line. When we earnestly started looking into selling our business, we made every decision with thoughts of how it affected the bottom line. We were able to make ourselves radically more valuable in such a short period of time, that it makes us wonder what could have been if we were always so aware.

Also, you need to have a product that is attractive and desirable. Whether it's your revenue, intellectual property, talented employees, large customer base, or business connections – you need to have something that is a desired commodity. We had each of those categories covered and thus were approached many times through the years for purchase.

5. Stay above petty emotional and personality conflicts

Managing employees and partner relationships is never easy. Humans are very emotional. My degree in Psychology gave me some insight into how people react and feel about situations, but there is no getting around the fact that some people are just not compatible with each other.

Having to smooth hurt feelings, diffuse anger, combat ineptness, and get everyone working as a team is very challenging. Sometimes I would get the feeling that I would be better off doing everything myself. But, as our business grew, that was not practical. I had to learn to give up control and to admit I wasn't the best man for every job.

More sage advice from my father of course: *Partnerships are a lot easier when there is little money.* As soon as you start making money, there are a lot more problems. I didn't believe that one at all! Isn't everyone happy when they are making good money? Yes and no.

True we were successful and started achieving our dreams early on. But, when you have to make distributions of profits, raises, etc.

that can't always be equal – things become strained. I learned that along with those issues – sometimes personal feelings can adversely affect partnerships. I know to keep business as business and personal life as personal life. But, some people have a distinctly different belief system and will not be able to get past negative feelings they have about others' behaviors.

It is best to keep your personal life as private as possible and do not let troubles away from work seep into the workplace.

6. Sell when the timing is right even if you are fearful

Selling was difficult. This business was my family. It was so much of my life. I truly loved work and looked forward to going in (most days!). I had to separate my feelings and make a business decision and remember what my goals were.

Selling the company culminated in the achievement of every one of my goals I had when I started it. The fear of having to come up with new goals and start a new phase of my career was daunting, but, I could not let that get in the way of making a good business decision.

Owning a business is such a rewarding experience. I relate it to raising children. There is so much pride and enjoyment achieved only with a lot of hard work and getting through tough times. Upon maturity it is time to let go and move on. It is hard to let go of your baby, but sometimes it is just the natural progression. You cannot let the fear of change or of the unknown cause inaction.

7. Design a new compelling future

I have learned so much through my experiences owning and running a business. I gained confidence, humility, friendships, insight, security, maturity - the list goes on and on. I know now that the lessons I learned from my parents as a child have immense value and I look forward to passing them on to my children.

Now I am starting on a new career that excites me but has also put me out of my comfort zone. It is never easy to start afresh but therein lies the joy of learning and mastering a new profession. I look forward to becoming a better business person and help more people with my knowledge and expertise.

About the Author:

Jeff Wright is available to teach business owners on how they can stay on top of their business and finances. He can be reached at (734) 259-9187 or at jeffrey.wright.llc@gmail.com.

Will You Get The Paycheck You Deserve?
5 Things You Can Do To Maximize Your Exit Strategy
By Rick Smith

Business owners draw a paycheck, an ongoing income, from their business for the hard work they put in, day in and day out. But very few business owners take into account the real paycheck they deserve that they may not have even planned for.

As a business broker, I have seen many people launch a successful business. Some planned very well and some just happened to accidentally get in business.

A professional friend always knew what kind of business he wanted to own. He wanted to own and operate his own CPA firm. A career like that requires significant education, internships and certification by the state board. He dutifully completed all of those steps and was hired by one of the large accounting firms in the area. He completed his assignments with them and then took the step to start his own firm, as he had planned. He is now known as the "Accountant to the Stars" in the greater Houston area working for many well-known celebrities. His business was created by having a well defined plan.

Whether you have a plan or not to start a business, you must plan for your exit strategy so you can get the biggest paycheck for all the blood, sweat and tears you have put into it.

I can tell you numerous stories about clients who have failed to plan their exit strategy and they received either less money at the time when they sold their business or realized that they could not sell the business because they had not taken some of the details into consideration.

Where Should Your Focus Be - Running or Selling Your Business?

I recently had a client that came to me after trying to sell his business on his own. While attempting to do that, he spent the majority of his time working with people that expressed an interest in the business. He had to spend time with all of them because he didn't know whether they were a qualified buyer or just a "tire kicker".

So guess what, while he was spending time doing that, he was taking time away from running his business. He now had to work harder to do both. And people would show up at the business unannounced asking his employees questions. Then his employees started asking him questions, and he had to make up stories that he wasn't really selling. It was a total disruption to his business and his life. And the worst part was, these distractions drove sales down, which devalued his business. He learned the value of planning and using a business broker the hard way.

He listed his business for sale with us. While doing that, he was able to run his business the way it should be run, which raised his sales again and created more value to potential buyers. We did the entire buyer screening using our qualification processes. We did all of the marketing. We did the pre-meetings with the buyer to explain the business in more detail so the buyer could determine if it was a good fit for them. We sat down with a qualified buyer and captured the initial terms of the purchase and then presented that to the seller and managed the negotiation process until a deal was reached. We then worked with all the parties to remove all of the contingencies on the deal, like completing a due diligence process and then getting the final legal documents done. Then we closed the transaction and the seller ended up with 15% more in his pocket even after paying the commission expense that was due to us.

You may be thinking, Rick, I am not planning to sell my business. It is possible that you plan to turn over the business to a family member or a friend. That could be a terrible mistake if not planned properly as the business transfer is seldom that easy.

Another client worked his whole life to build up his business to a very successful point. He thought he had an exit strategy, which was turning the business over to his son. His son didn't want to run the business. His dad was flabbergasted by the proclamation.

Obviously, there are a few things wrong with this whole picture, but the biggest thing is that his plan wasn't going to work. He ended up coming to us and we sold his business and he was able to retire, but it took him much longer than he had planned.

In this chapter, I want to first help you understand why it is important to have an exit strategy as early as possible in your career and what can you do to enhance the value of the business when you are ready to finance your golden years.

Create A Plan To Sell You Business

Selling a business correctly takes time. Be prepared to sell. Talk to your advisors, like your CPA or your business coach, and tell them what your intention is. Don't just think about your plan, write it down at a minimum in an outline form, just so you can visualize and track your progress to your plan. Your CPA will handle accounting entries differently if he knows you are planning to sell. He will make sure that all of the sales you generate are properly reflected and he will help you strengthen your balance sheet to make everything look as positive as possible.

As part of you planning process, get a valuation done on your business. That will create a benchmark for you. When the valuation is completed, you will know what areas of the business you can work on to create a higher value as you prepare to sell. For example, outstanding debt might need to be focused upon. Removing or reducing the debt will make your balance sheet look better, which creates more value.

Talk to a person that is knowledgeable about the selling process. Find an established Business Broker. Business Brokers are trained in the process of selling. Meet with a broker, way ahead of your intended sale date. Business brokers work with business owners everyday and they will explain the process of selling. They will talk about the proven ways to build value, find qualified buyers and also assist you with the entire selling process, from the first introductory meeting with them, to the actual closing of the transaction.

A good broker will manage the whole process on your behalf. They will set realistic expectations about many things, like:

- How long does it take to sell? How many potential buyers will I have to talk to? Will I get cash at closing?
- Will I have to finance any part of the transaction?
- How long will I have to train the new owner?
- When do I tell my employees that I am selling? Should I inform my landlord ahead of the actually sale?...and many more.

Have you asked the critical question, what would happen to your business if you were not around?

Remove Yourself From Daily Operations

If you are like most business owners, you got into the business to enjoy a better lifestyle. You want freedom from a boss, more money and the flexible hours of work. Unfortunately the daily grind of the business to create a cash flow takes the business owners' focus from more money and flexible hours to just plain more work.

Very few business owners have a systematic approach to running a business where you delegate as many jobs as possible so you can oversee the operations enough to know that the business is running smoothly and profitably.

At this time your goal should be to reach a point where your personal involvement is minimal so whether you are physically there or not, the business is still doing well.

This is the ideal scenario. Once you reach that phase, not only are you making money but you have peace of mind as well. Does this happen by accident? No, never!

Whether you plan to sell the business or not, wouldn't it be fun to know that you have created a cash-flow vehicle that runs without you?

Let me give you another example of what happened when an owner sold their business without a plan.

A $25,000 Mistake

A client came to us to buy a business because he just recently had sold his business. We asked him what kind of business it was and out of professionally curiosity, asked how much he sold it for. We knew generally what price that kind of business would bring, because we had sold several of them before. When he told us what he was paid, he noticed a puzzled look on our face. We asked him how the sale had come about.

One day, one of his customers approached him and asked him if he wanted to sell. He had known the person for a while, and he had thought of selling, but he didn't really have a price in mind. The buyer told him the price he was thinking about, and the seller thought that was fair, because after all, he started the business from nothing, so having a lump sum of money as he left sounded good to him. When we told him the business should have sold for at least $25,000 more, he cringed.

So how can you be prepared to sell when the moment arises?

There are five things you can do to enhance the value of the business and sell the business according to a plan.

1. Make the business independent of your personal involvement as much as possible
2. Consult a business broker early on to evaluate your business and keep him involved for guidance.
3. Create a plan as to when you would like to sell your business
4. Establish minimum expectations on what this business should bring to you. Have an understanding whether you will be part of the management team that will help transition the business.
5. Revisit your plan every year to find out how close you are to selling your business.

Plan for your sale, review your plan annually, and communicate your intentions to all who could be involved, get a valuation, and when you actually decide to sell, hire a Business Broker. Get the maximum amount of money for your business as you leave, because you deserve that biggest paycheck of all!

About the Author:

Rick Smith is an experienced, certified business broker and President of Summit Business Brokers. He has helped numerous business owners get their biggest paycheck by selling the business most efficiently and profitably. To get a $220.00 discount off the Regular $2,200.00 Business Valuation price, please call Rick and mention this book. Contact Rick at (248) 620-6754 or visit his web site at www.sbbmi.com

PART TWO
Marketing And Sales Makeover

Get The Competitive Edge By Raising Your Price
DR. BRYAN CORNWALL

Publicity: Find A True P.R. Angle And Get Promoted For Free
LISA LAPIDES SAWICKI

Marketer Of Marketing Shares Exclusive Marketing Secrets
PETE SWARTZ

Confused Prospects Never Buy
DR. SCOTT MCLEOD

Ten Ways To Add Sex Appeal To Your Business
TODD GULICH

The Referral Miracle: The Fable of the Magical Coins
CHARLES GIFFORD

Seven Matchmaking Tips: For Finding, Dating,
And Keeping Business Referral Partners
GAIL MICHELMAN AND LOUIS WEISS

Who Do I Know Strategy.... Who You Want To Know & Why!
NATALIE DeLEO

When to Pop The Question? Timing The Close
MINESH BAXI

5 Keys To Match Your Business Goals To Your Website
STEVE HYER

Building Your Business Brand Using Audio,
Web Video And Automated Sales Funnels
TED CANTU

Get the Competitive Edge by Raising Your Price
Secret to Best Veterinary Hospital in Clarkston
BY DR. BRYAN CORNWALL, D.V.M.

Do you believe your product or services have to be discounted in order to be competitive in your industry? Do you believe that due to the economic state people are unwilling to pay for quality products or services?

Nothing can be further from the truth.

We live in an era of discounted products and services. Our mailboxes are flooded with coupons and other circulars advertising products and services at discounted rates. The average business owner is lead to believe that in order to get a competitive edge they must discount their prices. This is a common misnomer!

Have you ever heard the phrase "you get what you pay for?" Well, this is oftentimes true with the plethora of discounts being offered. Many of these seemingly great deals are accompanied with small print "conditions" as well as products that lack quality. The average consumer is more apt to pay higher prices for quality products or services that meet or exceed his expectations than to deal with the conditions and poor quality of so many of the supposed "great deals."

Let's take as a hypothetical example a service we all use at some point or another, something simple, a car wash. We've all stumbled upon a $2.00 car wash here or there and immediately noticed that our vehicle was in desperate need of being washed. After a quick wash and pulling out of the car wash we realize that the $2.00 wash did not include towel drying. By the time we reach our destination we exit the car and after looking over the car we realize the car isn't as clean as we'd like it and now also has water spots.

Let's revisit the car wash concept. What if we'd stumbled upon a car wash that was $15.99 and made the stop, and after leaving we had a car wash that included an outside wash, an inside vacuum, inside windows, dashboard cleaned and a towel dry. When exiting the vehicle we see a very clean car and are happy.

Also there was a nice air-conditioned office where we could wait and be offered a beverage of our choice. Which one of these car washes would the discerning consumer prefer? Well of course, the latter because they have received quality service and did not mind paying for it.

There is a market for high end products and services.

I am equipped with this knowledge from personal experience. I am a Veterinarian and owner of a high end pet care hospital. After working in private practice I was determined to build a practice that had a reputation for providing excellent care, outstanding customer service, integrity, and reliability all delivered with empathy and compassion. It was not an easy road as I had much to learn about hiring and training the right staff. However, because of the dedication to providing excellent service to our customers more than they expected our business immediately received phenomenal growth. Because of our commitment to being the best, over the past sixteen years we have grown to be well respected not only in the community but also by our colleagues.

At Advanced PetCare of Oakland, we are not only known for our love and care of animals but our understanding of the relationships between pets and their owners. Our genuine concern for the pets and their owners is displayed at all times. Pet owners know that when they bring their pets to us we will treat the pet as if it were our own. In addition to providing exceptional service to pets we serve our clients by valuing their relationship with their pets. Providing such service has caused our facility to be the best in our area with growth not seen by others.

You too can have the same success.

First you must identify the processes in becoming a high end product or service provider. How do you position your business as a provider of Quality Service or Products?

Let's identify some components to gaining the competitive edge
1. SERVICE
Service is the most important component of quality. How do

you provide exceptional service? Let's start with identifying your competitors. Visit the competitors and evaluate their service and figure out what was lacking and how you can implement those features in the service of your business. Some simple techniques to offering exceptional quality service are:

- Learn your customer's names and address them accordingly. People like personalized service.
- Send thank you notes.
- Send announcements or newsletters and let your customers know what's going on.
- Ask your clients/customers for feedback to help improve your service.
- Be sincere and genuine in offering quality service. People can distinguish between genuine service and rehearsed or mandated quality service.

2. DELIVERY

Delivery is another crucial component of quality service. Do you deliver the product or service as you claim? Can you stand by your product or service and your claim to be the best?

- Delivery as it relates to quality is defined by the WOW factor. Your clients/customers should be "Wowed" by the end product. Consumers build loyalty when their expectations are met and especially when they are exceeded.
- Deliver the product on time, without excuses. Consumers want what they pay for and they don't like being given the runaround. If possible deliver before expected.
- Deliver the product or service with sincere gratitude and appreciation.

3. CREATE A FRIENDLY ENVIRONMENT

Creating a friendly environment goes above and beyond great customer service. By creating a friendly environment your customers will become loyal to you based on the environment and service. Little things can make your customers feel valued and appreciated, such as fresh coffee and donuts while they wait.

Make sure your environment represents your quest to have the competitive edge.

- Create an environment so friendly your customers are reluctant to leave.
- By creating an environment full of comfort and ease your clients will become accustomed to being pampered. A friendly environment means your customers feel "extra special" throughout their entire experience. By creating such an environment customers are afraid to take their business elsewhere due to the fear that the service and friendly environment cannot be matched.

4. FOLLOW UP

Follow up is essential as it relates to quality. Whatever your product or service is, it is important to implement a system that maintains continuous communication with customers. There are several ways to implement exceptional follow up.

- Send thank you notes to your customers, or make follow up thank you calls to ensure the customer has received the best experience.
- Send announcements, newsletters, and any other pertinent information to your customers.
- Keep records of customers and how often they visit. Make calls or send postcards to customers that you have not seen in a while.

Providing exceptional quality products or services is enough to gain a competitive edge. You don't have to discount your prices, just ensure your customers are getting more than they pay for in terms of value.

At Advanced PetCare of Oakland we do just that. We provide exceptionally quality service to our customers. We also pride ourselves on having the latest equipment. Our fully trained staff is afforded continuing education opportunities to ensure a staff that is equipped with all the cutting edge knowledge. We believe in giving back to the community and do so regularly. We offer dog and cat CPR classes, dog training academies held in our lobby once a week, and dog washes. The community is very supportive of our community events and we build lasting relationships with customers and potential customers through these events.

Customers/clients don't mind paying for exceptional products and services. They'd rather pay a higher price once than to spend the time correcting errors from poor quality products or service. The average consumer understands the value of time and they understand that their time is worth the money. With this understanding in mind they would prefer paying for the service or product they want than to waste their valuable time.

So don't fall prey to the common misnomer that you have to offer discounted products and services to be competitive. Raise your price and your quality service and get the competitive edge you are seeking. Remember to continuously find new ways to implement exceptional service and keep your clients informed of all the exciting things you have going on. Word of mouth has always proven to be a great marketing tool, and when a customer is excited about the service they have received they are sure to recommend your business to a friend or family member. What better way to increase your business?

About the Author:

Dr. Bryan M. Cornwall – Owner, Advanced PetCare of Oakland Dr. Cornwall is recognized for his complex diagnostic and surgical skills. Prior to opening his hospital in 1992, Dr. Cornwall practiced at other Detroit area veterinary and emergency centers. He graduated with high honors from Michigan State University College of Veterinary Medicine in 1989, where he received awards for excellence in clinical and surgical skills. Dr. Cornwall also received the Ziegler Caring Award as selected by his classmates. He is an active member in the Southeastern Michigan Veterinary Medical Association, Michigan Veterinary Medical Association, American Veterinary Medical Association, and the American Animal Hospital Association. Dr. Cornwall is married, has two daughters and five cats. His office can be reached at (248) 620-2900

Publicity: Find a True P.R. Angle
And Get Promoted For Free

By Lisa Lapides Sawicki

One of the most effective marketing tools any business can employ is publicity. Attracting the positive attention of any media outlet (radio, television, newspaper, magazine, webzine, blogger, etc.) can give business a boost. Publicity may be less expensive than traditional advertising and the results are easier to successfully track. Based on more than twenty years of experience assisting all manner of clients in attracting the media spotlight, I want to share some observations and tips on how to package and pitch your story idea to an assignment editor or reporter.

Most professionals understand that "Advertising – you pay for and Publicity – you pray for".

. The biggest benefit of publicity is that you can get exposure in your target market area and attract the aura of being a credible expert. In the defining moment when a prospect has to make a decision of whether he should choose you over your competition, this could be the stark difference between getting the contract and failing to get one.

Publicity is a very powerful marketing tool that you can leverage to get the type of exposure you desire to gain valuable clients and build a portfolio that can be the envy of your competition.

A word of caution: favorable publicity is rarely achieved overnight and that is the reason why I have listed these observations and tips for your benefit.

1. **Have a clear picture of whom you are addressing:** Who is the potential audience for your particular message? Are they men or women, teens or kids, what are their ages, economic or education levels, interests, cultures? Which media outlets are these people drawn to? Which reporters at these outlets have done similar types of stories (this may be their particular area of expertise or

"beat")? The majority of journalists report exclusively about a single topic; business, health, family, sports, entertainment, etc. Having an idea of who covers which particular areas and what they have recently reported can also add to your confidence when it comes time to call that person and inquire directly about a press release you have submitted.

2. **Tune in to the national dialogue:** What are hot topics of the moment? If your story can be positioned as adding some fresh piece of information or perspective on a topic that is currently making headlines, it will make it much easier to gain a journalist's attention. Or, if your story can take a large, complex issue and help break it down and simplify it, that can work, too. (For example, illustrating creative solutions that people are using to conserve gasoline in the face of higher fuel prices, or finding innovative ways to trim a grocery bill to deal with rising food prices.)

3. **Brainstorm with someone beyond your business:** If you plan to manage your own publicity, it may still be a good investment to hire a PR professional or secure a few hours with someone whom you respect to brainstorm your angle and intended message. Keep in mind that sometimes we are so close to our own enterprises that we can miss a great idea that is obvious to an outsider. If you are not at ease with writing, consider hiring a professional to craft your press release.

4. **Track the trends in your industry:** Stay up to date by reading trade publications, paying attention to individual reporters and columnists, their theories and opinions, and current advertising, too. Presenting your story as an industry trend that hasn't yet reached mainstream media can help get attention.

5. **Find data or statistics that supports your angle:** Statistics will always help move your story. It always adds credibility to your headline or press release when you use industry statistics or data

to support your angle. Now we can use the Internet to search for information that supports your angle, your point, or your cause. Tap into industry associations as well. Many associations post data on their websites. Reporters need to justify "placing" your angle / press release in their morning meetings with their managing editor.

6. **Be a bearer of good news:** It is a sad truth that on most days, journalists have their choice of less than positive stories to cover. Providing an inspiring alternative may help you gain their attention.

7. **Be an expert, or at least a trusted advisor:** There is an old adage that he, who first declares himself to be an expert, becomes one. If this is beyond your level of comfort, seek to establish an honest, ongoing rapport with reporters covering your beat, they may seek you out time and again for your considered opinion. Professional publicists are very often important story resources for busy reporters.

8. **Know the weight of your message:** Appreciate the difference in importance between a new management hire and a new staff person added. Understand when your message is more suitable for a brief mention than a full article, and don't request broader coverage than it deserves. On the flip side, if you think your message is universal enough to warrant regional, national or international attention, consider using a wire service such as PR Newswire to disseminate it to all available media. The additional cost can be well worth the investment.

9. **Be empathetic to the reality of being a journalist today:** Changes in media usage, diminishing and shifting ad budgets are resulting in some very lean staff rosters. Many journalists today are stretched to stay on top of all the releases that come their way, which may number hundreds each day. When placing your follow up phone calls, expect that they may not have read your release and plan to resend. It's appreciated. Don't leave more than two messages. It is as annoying to them as it would be to you. When they do answer their phone, inquire if they have a moment before launching into your pitch.

Again, the courtesy is appreciated. Be very clear about why your story may be of interest to their particular audience. Keep good notes about each beat or reporter's regular deadlines and planning cycles and honor them whenever possible. Every media outlet is different.

10. **Be accessible:** Phone calls from news media should be handled as top priority. Like it or not, "no comment" or an unreturned news media phone call is a powerful message. Many PR firms have a 15-minute "call back" policy. When handling your own publicity, a similar guideline should be followed.

11. **Be concise:** When it comes to press releases, more content is not necessarily better. This is not a creative writing exercise. Keep it to one page, make sure all the pertinent info is in the lead paragraph, and include limited quotes. Make sure your phone number and email are included and correct. Avoid editorializing (making unsubstantiated claims of greatness). Trust me; they've heard it all before. If they would like to learn more, they'll contact you.

12. **Include photos or graphics:** If you can illustrate your message visually, it helps! Reader attention spans and time spent with individual media are shrinking. Always include a photo credit and caption with photos.

How to do a great interview:
- Know your topic inside and out. Do your homework. Write out 6-8 key points prior to the interview.
- Practice whatever techniques that work for you to control frustration and nervousness. The best interviews are from those that appear comfortable with whom they are. (Deep breathing really helps, mental rehearsals and practicing in front of a mirror works great as well.)
- Don't use notes unless it's absolutely necessary. You are supposed to be the expert. Using notes obstructs the flow of the interview.
- Always make good eye contact with the host / reporter.
- Keep the energy level up. Speak with enthusiasm and conviction.

Treat the interview as an "important conversation" that's must be very precise.
- Never give one-word answers. There's nothing more frustrating and boring than an interview that won't talk.
- Don't wear very light colors or busy patterns on television.
- Speak to the camera when answering a question, look at the interviewer when asking one.
- Try to always get a copy of your interview so afterwards, you can critique yourself.
- Know your topic inside and out (worth repeating).

13. **How to Handle Bad News:** What's the best way to handle bad news when you're dealing with the press? First, be honest and direct. Second, be honest and direct. Third, be honest and direct. Fourth, do not hide. The worst thing you can do in a crisis or other bad situation is to say "no comment." Regardless of the situation, "no comment" makes you look guilty of something. Fifth, be available to answer questions. Don't speculate. "Guesses," observations, and conjecture can be misinterpreted as facts that might haunt you later. (Beckwith, Streetwise Complete Publicity Plans).

14. **Track your results:** Good publicity can serve your business for years to come. A company can repeatedly use their publicity clippings. There is no expiration date! If you are planning a wide press release or anticipating heavy interest in your story, consider hiring a clipping service and/or video monitoring service so that you don't miss any articles or segments that run. Given the rapid pace of media these days, it is not at all unusual for an outlet to pick up your release and photo and run it verbatim without contacting you. This happens every day!

15. **Now, use your publicity to "sell" and gain credibility:** When you do garner media attention, share it with the world! Include it in a newsletter, post it on your website, include it in your sales portfolio, hang it on the wall! An editorial placement is

invaluable because it simply cannot be bought. The independent, objective review of media generally carries much greater weight and credibility with consumers than any advertising you might purchase.

About the Author:

Lisa Lapides Sawicki, founder of Lapides Publicity Giragosian is available for publicity workshops, speaking engagements, and publicity campaigns. To get a free 25 minute customized and personal phone consultation on "What Is Your P.R. Angle" contact her at (248) 399-8200 or by e-mail at LPGroup@sbcglobal.net.

Marketer of Marketing Shares Exclusive Marketing Secrets

By Pete Swartz

When consulting with clients I've found most business owners have phenomenal products and services but lack the knowledge and understanding on how to effectively market the business. Reading this chapter will lead to a complete mental makeover on the concept of marketing inevitably leading to highly successful marketing campaigns.

The direct response marketing concepts shared in this chapter are used by some of the world's most successful businesses. These proven strategies can be implemented for any size business to generate desired end results.

I've outlined some common problems I've heard from business owners;
1. They have no idea what type of marketing strategy to implement for their specific type of business.
2. They outsource marketing to marketing professionals but have no idea what their return on investment is.
3. They assume that once they started a business and made it visible to consumers they'd have an influx of customers/clients.

I have been an entrepreneur since graduating high school. My dad owned a construction business and I worked side by side with him learning the ins and outs of owning and operating a business. I always tell people that I have a degree from Live and Learn University. I've heard others say they have attended the school of Hard Knocks, however I prefer to use "live and learn." That phrase works best for me because it transcends my journey over the years. Throughout my career, I've lived but most importantly I've LEARNED.

I have over the years utilized my natural talents to successfully develop and prosper in many businesses including; a day care center, a bed and breakfast, a wholesale painter's supply outlet, and an antique business, to name a few. Currently I am the owner of an extremely successful building and land development company. I thoroughly understand what it takes make a business successful through direct response marketing and have a passion to teach others.

During the course of this chapter you will receive the necessary, already proven, successful marketing strategies that will empower you on your quest for 30 Day Total Business Makeover. These strategies can be specifically applied to your business. Reading this chapter will undoubtedly leave you with information that will cause you to think differently about marketing as it relates to your business. Knowledge is power and I will empower you with the knowledge to change your marketing strategies.

What do all business owners hate?

We HATE being advertising victims. By that I mean, wasting money. Not knowing exactly what to do. Listening to ad media salespeople who convince us to buy their advertising whether it works for us or not. We hate not knowing where our next customers are coming from. We hate all this uncertainty. And, we hate feeling like we can't compete.

How are these issues resolved?

Taking an active role in marketing your business with a complete comprehension of marketing concepts, and implementing these proven concepts will alleviate being victimized by marketing plans that don't generate results. The first thing to understand is it doesn't matter what type of business you own and operate, the business that you are REALLY in is the Advertising, Marketing, and Sales business.

Are you ready for a life changing marketing makeover? As an independent business advisor for Dan Kennedy, I am going to share a proven marketing system with you. This style of marketing system;

1. Works in any media
   a. direct mail
   b. email
   c. advertising
   d. print

e. voice broadcasting
f. internet marketing
g. web 2.0
2. Can effectively track the return on investment.

There are three basic components to the direct response marketing system as outlined which include the marketing message, target marketing and media.

Marketing Message

The marketing message is defined as the message that gets the consumer's attention. It is the message that reaches out and explains to your potential customer the following;
1. Who you are.
2. Why they should trust you with their business.
3. Why they should choose you over your competitors.

All marketing messages should be the answer to an emotional need. What problem is the potential customer having and how can you provide a solution to that problem? One of the best marketing messages I've seen which resulted in extreme success for the creators is Dominos Pizza's "fresh, hot pizza delivered in 30 minutes or less, guaranteed."

Let's take a minute to analyze the components of this marketing message. The message identifies a need - the customer is hungry. It solves a problem by guaranteeing that the product will be hot and it will be delivered within thirty minutes. It gives a competitive edge by guaranteeing a promise.

As seen by the Domino's example every marketing message should contain a promise and a meaningful specific, and a guarantee. This is known as a *positioning statement*.

Marketing messages should also contain PROOF. You are better served having your customers or clients tell your story for you. Every place you aren't using testimonials is a place you should. If you do nothing else as a result of reading this material, start using great testimonials everywhere, this will make a measurable difference.

After you have composed a marketing message you must understand that this message is not for everyone. It is only, and I repeat only, for your target market. In order for your marketing message to work it must be delivered to your specific target market.

Target Marketing

Target marketing starts with the target, NOT your product or service or business. It starts with: WHO? Who is your ideal prospect? Where are they? That's simple geography and a lot of people get that far. But demographics and psychographics are more important. It is important to figure out WHO we want; get a list of them or craft advertising that calls out just to them and attracts them When you stop throwing slop at everybody, mud against the wall, and start zeroing in like a laser beam on the right "who," you get better results.

Trying to find your specific target market will require some intense research depending on your product or service. However, it is very important that you invest the time to find out where your potential clients are. You want to find out who needs your product and where to reach them. Once you find where they are you want to begin a marketing campaign geared to them.

When you deliver your marketing message to your target market you will generate results. If you own a daycare you wouldn't want to waste your money sending advertisements to people that don't have any children. It's as simple as that. Target marketing is finding consumers that need your product or service.

Media

All media could be good media, newspapers, magazines, or whatever. However, most people approach marketing with random acts. In a sloppily hit or miss oftentimes under pressure approach. It is imperative to understand that Direct Response Marketing works!

Infomercials are great examples of direct response marketing media. Infomercials identify a need and provide a resolution to the need and for the generally provide some type of guarantee. Customers respond directly by calling in to order the product that poses a solution to their problem.

With direct response media the consumer directly responds to an offer for a product or service. It emotionally motivates them to understand a particular problem they are facing and see that there is an immediate solution.

Generally when direct mail tactics are mentioned people say they've tried it before and it doesn't work in their business. Direct mail is just one media and the same can be applied to multi-media such as email, advertising and voice broadcasting. When direct response mail tactics are used the end results include name-brand recognition as well as immediate profitable response.

Direct response marketing WORKS! It has worked continuously for me and countless of other businesses, and it will work for you too! You must first understand the methodology behind direct response marketing and then you can implement it into any marketing campaign you desire and watch it work. Direct response marketing is a systematic approach to generating maximum results.

Remember you must first perform due diligence as previously stated and know why a prospect should choose to do business with you over anyone else. You must know your target market and streamline your marketing to people in need of your product or service. You must understand media and how advertising works in order to effectively understand your return on investment as it relates to your marketing dollars. Implementing the direct response marketing system into your business strategies will definitely put you on the right path to a 30 Day Total Business Makeover.

About the Author:

Pete Swartz is known as the Marketer of Marketing. Pete's years of experience and expertise has earned him the guru status. Pete works as an independent marketing advisor for Dan Kennedy. Pete teaches this marketing module at local Chamber of Commerce business meetings throughout the Metropolitan Detroit area. More information about Pete Swartz and the direct response marketing strategies can be found online at www.oaklandcounty-gkic.com.

Get "*The Most Incredible Free Gift Ever*" when you visit the website.

Confused Prospects Never Buy
Creating Lifetime Clients with Educational Marketing
By Dr. Scott McLeod

I received a phone call from a young Dr. Thomas late one summer evening. He was a struggling chiropractor who had recently started a family and a practice. What I heard on the other end of the line however, was a voice filled with fear and distress.

"I found your name on the internet" he said, "and I was wondering if you could help out a fellow doctor in need." I love helping people so I asked him to explain.

As our conversation unfolded, I learned that he was, in fact, a new doctor who was dealing with a mounting financial crisis. The crisis was created by a combination of mounting bills from building a new practice, starting a new family, and his student loans coming due. The stress was overwhelming and controlling every moment of his life. He was frightened... very frightened.

He was afraid that everything he had worked for in Chiropractic College might soon come to an end as he might have to close the doors of his newly established practice. He was reaching out, and what he found was me, a chiropractor who appeared to have successfully conquered the transition from student to doctor, from novice to expert, from intern to entrepreneur.

What he didn't know however, was that this transition didn't happen suddenly for me. In fact my success took time, trials and mistakes. It took an eventual unwavering commitment to helping others understand what I could truly offer them.

I shared with him that evening, what I thought his best chance for survival was. What I told him is the same thing I hope to give to you. The secret of creating a successful business of growth, stability and prosperity... Educational Marketing.

- Would you like to have more business?
- Would you like to spend less money attracting new clients?
- Would you like to retain your current clients for a lifetime and

have them refer new business to you?

If you answered yes to any of these questions then read on.

Allow me to introduce myself. My name is Dr. Scott McLeod, and I am a practicing doctor in the field of chiropractic care. I have been involved with the chiropractic profession for almost 20 years. I have helped many people learn how to grow their business through simple, yet powerful principles that I would now like to share with you.

This chapter is going to show you how, through educational marketing, to not only get new clients, but to also satisfy those clients, and retain them for a lifetime.

Isn't it true that the majority of people who seek your product or service don't really know the full extent of what you have to offer them? For example, in my profession, most people who seek out chiropractic care, in fact don't really even know *what chiropractic is*. They may think they understand it, but in fact over 95% of the people I see (whether they have had previous chiropractic experience or not) have a misunderstanding of what my profession is and how much I have to offer.

So, in order to correct this problem, I have made it a priority of mine to **educate each and every patient who seeks my care**... and it begins *before* they even enter my office.

Educational Marketing

Every business owner knows the importance of marketing to generate business. However, many times marketing is done to simply get new people in the door. This type of marketing can be very expensive and only moderately successful at best. Examples may range from print ads in newspapers and the yellow pages to direct mail promotions, billboards, radio and/or cable advertising. This type of marketing can create new customers, yet these consumers may come with false expectations and a misunderstanding of what service you may offer.

For example, in my profession many well meaning chiropractors will advertise "pain relief" in a print ad to attract new patients. The reason for this is because pain (such as back or neck pain) is a common indicator for underlying problems that chiropractors can correct, and in doing so, can offer relief. Like the oil light on your car's dashboard. The light may be irritating to look at, but it is only a symptom of what the actual problem is... low oil! Would it make sense for a mechanic to advertise "red light relief"? Only if he is looking for a short term client who only wants to rid himself of the red light syndrome. Then, the mechanic can simply put a piece of tape over the light and charge an insignificant fee to the auto owner as a red light elimination service.

The downside is obvious. In the example of the automobile, the oil level will continue to drop and the engine will eventually freeze up and cease to operate leaving the auto owner with anger and a lack of transportation.

The patient who sees a pain relief ad may make an appointment to see that chiropractor and expect to receive pain relief only with no intention of the real benefit... correcting the cause of their problem.

One of the ways that I have attempted to avoid this problem is to always advertise my intent... **Correct The Cause**! I have a very educational website which is designed to start this process. This intent is declared boldly both in my logo and in my website address.

In fact, I include my website in all of my forms of advertisements, business cards, stationary and everything that has my name on it. This way, instead of trying to get them "in the door", we allow them to enter the very non-confrontational environment of our virtual office online. This allows the prospective patients to get introduced to us and learn what they can expect when they come into our office before their first time.

The web address itself presets the patient's mindset into a proper paradigm. For example, I could have chosen from any number of different options like www.GetOutOfPainNow.com, or www.

PainRelief.com, etc., but instead I chose www.CorrectTheCause.com.

"Correct The Cause" sets the standard of my care before they even see me.

Once a person visits my website, **the education process begins**. By simply watching online videos, reading short explanations of what to expect, and downloading paperwork, the new patient is prepped, and ready to begin. This process, known as stimulating the senses, includes predominantly three forms of communication- one of which most people use as their primary method of communicating. These three forms include visual, auditory, and kinesthetic. Visual people need to see things in order for them to understand. People who utilize auditory methods of communicating need to hear the spoken word or carry on a conversation. Kinesthetic communication involves responding more to touch and feelings. It is important to try to incorporate all three forms of communication in the educational marketing process to get the best results.

5 Simple Steps to Educational Marketing

1. <u>Display your intent on every piece of marketing you use.</u>
Stop the revolving door method of getting new clients. Sure, cheap ad slogans may have the potential of getting you instant business, but when used without, or even in opposition to your intent, the results may be less than appealing. Chances are you will only receive short term customers and long term expenses.

Instead, put your best foot forward and be proud of your intentions. Be up front with your potential customers and they will appreciate you for it.

2. <u>Treat each person as an intelligent individual who deserves to be informed and educated about the products or services you can offer them.</u>
People deserve to be treated with intelligence and respect. However, they may not know, understand or appreciate the full extent of what you have to offer. Take the time to explain it to them, they will appreciate it.

For example, take the difference between a fast food restaurant and a fine dining establishment. Fast food restaurants offer cheap food fast. Their intent is clear; enter, order, and eat. Even their seating isn't designed to be comfortable for long stays. However, at a fine dining restaurant you will find the opposite. The atmosphere is designed around the quality of the food *and* the service. The wait staff takes time to educate those who are dining. Not only do they list the chef's specials for the day, but they take the opportunity to explain in detail how they are prepared. The seating is comfortable and the stay is relaxed. The result? A truly fine dining experience with return customers and referrals.

If you choose to offer the "fast food" type of service, that's fine. Otherwise give your customers the service that would be expected in the "fine dining" environment. Take the time to explain and educate your customers so they can make the best decisions regarding their business relationship with you.

3. Pre-educate your clients before they even enter your facility.
Do you have a website? If so, does it give your potential clients a chance to "visit" your facility without the fear of actually entering it? Virtual tours and explanations of what people should expect can tear down the walls of apprehension that your potential clients may have.

4. Take every opportunity to explain your products and/or services involving all of their senses.
People communicate in different ways. Would you try to speak Spanish to someone who only knew English? It can be difficult to identify someone's communication method upon first meeting them, so use them all. They will hear your message more clearly.

5. Re-educate on an ongoing basis.
Do yourself a favor and create stability for your business. Don't focus on obtaining new customers only, but grasp the concept of creating lifetime fans as well! These fans will not only stick around with you for the long term, but will refer others to you for years to come.

Does It Work?

Years later, I contacted Dr. Thomas and asked him how his practice was coming along. He stated that since he eliminated his old methods of revolving door marketing and implemented my suggestions of educational marketing, his practice has been flourishing. He now has a successful practice filled with people whom he has educated and served to the best of his ability. This, in turn, has created for him a solid foundation of lifetime fans! His fans continually refer a constant stream of new patients to him. Never again will he have the stress, fear and anxiety that I first heard in his voice during that first conversation we had on that late summer evening.

Educational Marketing can give you the same success and security!

About the Author

Dr. Scott McLeod is founder of McLeod Chiropratic & Wellness Center. To get your education process started, visit www. CorrectTheCause.com. Dr. McLeod is an excellent speaker and provides valuable seminars on health and building a strong business.

Ten Ways To Add Sex Appeal To Your Business
By Todd Gulich

So … I run an automotive repair facility in Waterford, Michigan. Yeah, I know – pretty exciting – isn't it? In the traditionally male-dominated and not very well publicly-favored automotive repair industry, we have taken notice of some consumer trends, and have implemented some simple marketing tools that are distinctly "gender-biased" into our business. These tools have significantly impacted the growth of our client base while raising some eyebrows. Similar implementation of some of these same tools may very well help you give your business a 30-day makeover!

Before we start to address the issue of adding **sex appeal** to your business, let me ask you; Are you *allowing* yourself, and your business, to adapt and adjust to today's ever-changing business climate? Are you *focusing* on the changes occurring in your marketplace? Can you name *one key shift* that has occurred in your client base over the last twelve months? What would happen to your business if your client base underwent a major transformation - and you missed it?

There is a significant paradigm shift occurring in the world marketplace, more specifically for our discussion, in the North American economy, that has been picking up steam over the last forty years. This trend has created one of the biggest buying segments of our population and it has become a formidable force in industries throughout the economy.

What is this paradigm shift? Here is a short excerpt from a Business Week article:

> **"Rising female consumer power is changing the way companies design, make and market products – and it's about more than adding pastels."**

Who is the apple of the marketing guru's eye? It is not those free-spending teens or men aged 25 – 50 years old. It is **women!** Thanks to their one-two punch of purchasing power and decision-making authority, working women in the ages of 24 to 54 years old – of whom the U.S. has some 55 million – have emerged as a very potent force in the marketplace. So potent, that their influence is changing the way companies design, position and sell their products more than any other demographic.

Even while women generally earn less than their male counterparts – 78 cents for every dollar a man gets, they make more than 80% of the buying decisions in all homes. And, women shop very differently from the way men do. Females research more extensively and are less likely to be influenced by superficial ads. 'Today's woman is the chief purchasing agent of the family and marketers have to recognize that,' says Michael Silverstein, principal at Boston Consulting Group and author of *Trading Up: The New American Luxury*."

The Employment Policy Foundation says the number of women earning $100,000 or more has tripled in the last ten years. There are women's organizations in almost every community supporting local women in business. There seems to be a constant flow of local seminars and educational opportunities for women to improve their financial savvy and management skills.

If all of this makes sense, then we need to pay more direct attention to how we are communicating to the women that may be present in the receiving audience of our marketplace.

That means we may need to take another look at our lobbies, retail and work space environment, our printed marketing materials, radio and cable ads, our website content, etc. We may need to rethink through what we say and how we deliver our message in every venue that we use to market ourselves, our company, products and services.

That may sound like a rather larger undertaking – especially considering the possible expense involved, the time required, the manpower necessary to implement these changes! Not so! These changes do not have to involve major expense, significant time commitment, or manpower. More accurately, they simply require changing behavior (and ultimately corporate culture) and/or redistributing marketing dollars to focus on those emotions, those items, those venues, that appeal to women and that move them to feel or realize that what you have to offer satisfies their wants or needs.

To start, let's talk about **you**. Do you make it a point to address women by their name in conversations and when greeting them? Dale Carnegie said that an individual's favorite word to hear is one's own name. I would suggest that addressing an individual by her name also subconsciously communicates to them that you have a personal interest in knowing who she is. If so, then what does it communicate when you **do not** use an individual's name to address them? This is a simple change in behavior, that won't cost you a penny. Yet, I guarantee that it will help you to communicate respect and develop an affinity with your female listening audience, whether they are your clients, associates or partners, that otherwise would not exist.

Here are ten simple strategies to improve the feminine appeal of your business that can generate immediate impact. Please note that these tips are coming from a male perspective.

1) **Add a feminine touch to the environment**.
Put live flowers and plants in entrance and waiting areas - even synthetic plants can add color! Greenery is soothing. Women enjoy pretty surroundings so keep live plants watered and vibrant.

Have background music playing that is calming and intelligent. Oftentimes female vocals and easy-listening or classical music can create a more relaxing environment for many women. In our facility, classical music delivers a sense of calm to a situation (i.e. car repairs) that is often more tense for women than it is for men.

You can use pictures to create a different impression or atmosphere also. I have an attorney friend (John) who has done some estate planning for our family. When my wife met John for the first time, it was in his office conference room where the walls are a neutral color lined with pictures of airplanes – I think they are actually his business partner's pictures. After the meeting, Dawn expressed that she found John to be "cold and business-like." Now, I know John to be a warm, friendly and comical guy, and he seemed very normal to me on that day. I wonder, would Dawn have perceived him differently if we had met in a room decorated with flowers or pastel prints, or maybe a window to an atrium? Yeah, I think so.

2) Keep the environment clean and bright.
Keep the environment clean and crisp, especially bathrooms, dressing rooms or any areas where she may be even partially disrobing. For many women, cleanliness is comforting. Our female clients often comment that we have the "cleanest bathroom in a car shop" that they have ever been in. Is that a competitive edge? You bet.

3) Educate and communicate.
Women are intelligent and they want to be treated as intelligent consumers. Look for opportunities to respectfully communicate and educate. If you provide pertinent product/service information, you will win her confidence in your delivery of those goods and eliminate fears of a potential bad buying decision.

In the automotive repair business, our parts and labor warranties provide an assurance of future care in the event of future problems. The longer the term of the warranty and the greater the coverage, the more implied durability in the parts and the repair. Thus, the more perceived value there is when buying from us. This can be applied to return policies, contingent care agreements, leases, retainers, contracts, etc. First communicate the details. Then, be sure to follow through if called upon to honor your word in the event of a future issue.

4) Keep your word on pricing.
Make pricing clear and visible and don't change the bottom line, unless she has pre-approved. With increased wherewithal and buying power, women are taking on more household and corporate fiscal responsibility. Women don't like to be fooled and they don't like to be taken for fools – especially about their money. I suggest that your integrity in product or service pricing, and communication about it is much more of a hot-button for women than it is for men. Respect her hard-earned income.

Women enter our auto repair shop, usually with some trepidation about the repairs needing to be done. To tell her that the bill came out higher than originally quoted virtually destroys her trust, unless we previously communicated the reasons why and got her prior approval.

5) Respect the intelligence of your female clientele.

Be professional in communication. Watch your language. Ask questions, ask permission, and ask for the sale. And listen, a lot! I suggest – that women love and need to be heard, probably more than men do. To run them over with your sales agenda is more of the same that they have dealt with most of their lives. Take care of their needs by asking what is important to them, how they want it delivered, and how they want to pay.

6) Be professional with women.

Be professional in your attire. Clothes are important to women – on you and on them. If you're a male, don't look like the guy that tried to hit on them in the grocery store or the bar last night. They will tend to immediately lose the trust factor.

7) Provide assurance and minimize uncertainty/fear.

Whatever you do ... do what you say you are going to do! Create more assurance and less uncertainty for your female clientele. I once heard someone say that people generally get upset for three primary reasons: 1) lack of communication about an issue; 2) unmet expectations; and, 3) uncertainty. If women are more emotional creatures, then instill behavior in your employees and corporate culture that creates more trust and less uncertainty on possibly the largest buying segment of your business.

What **NOT** to do:	Result:	What to do:	Result:
No communication	Uncertainty and Fear.	Extra phone call	Trust.
Broken promises	Uncertainty and Fear.	Follow-through	Trust.
Lie	Uncertainty and Fear.	Admission of fault	Trust.

8) Recognize their friends and their network.
When women appreciate you and your business, they refer their friends. When that happens, you need to acknowledge that referral with a phone call or a verbal thank you. Just simple recognition goes a long way to building a stronger bond in your relationship.

Deborah Micek, founder of WomenEntrepreneur.com, wrote on her website on 09/21/07, "When your customer grows to depend on you for whatever she needs, wants and desires – and tells her friends and family about you, your product and service – you've got yourself a loyal customer for life."

9) Follow-up the sale/service with more care.
A follow-up phone call or thank you letter also helps to generate more relationship. Women seem to want more relationship than men do. By providing added attention and acknowledgement, without solicitation for future business, you can build a more genuine and caring relationship.

In our business, we will often call a client to confirm that a repair was done properly with no further issues. This builds an ongoing relationship based on caring and assurance.

10) Conclude the sale/service with a bonus gift to say "Thank you."
Simple things like a flower(s), a bottle of water, a coupon, a gift card – again appeal to her as being special. Help them to feel special and they will treat you and your business as special.

In our business, a rose on the driver's seat is a nice touch for a lot of women clients. A small gift card for a local convenience store puts a smile on many-a-face. We offer to our female clients to take home the magazine they didn't get to finish while they were waiting for us to finish servicing their car – so simple yet so appreciated.

Here is a bonus tip: Be known as a charitable organization.
Women are more interested in supporting causes in the community than some men are; and they seem to recognize those organizations that participate in the programs that their children are involved in.

Supporting local children's hockey and football programs, community fund-raising events, and women's outreach programs have also helped us to maintain a community-oriented image and thus a growing clientele.

I would suggest that no matter who *you* are, your business is probably more about taking care of people through a product or a service, than it is anything else. In the automotive repair business, we fix and maintain cars, on the surface. Our underlying commitment is to take care of our clients by helping them to transport their families safely, travel efficiently, get to their employment on time, and enjoy their oftentimes long commute time.

Statistically, the percentage of women coming in automotive repair facilities across the country has risen from below 50% in the 1990's to almost 60% today. I would recommend that you continue to think further outside your box and entertain ideas of broadening the feminine appeal of your business. Step-up, serve them and enjoy the fruits of serving a very loyal and dedicated clientele, the female.

About the Author:

Todd S. Gulich is the happy husband of Dawn and the loving father of three beautiful girls, Laurissa, Caroline-Daisy and Lainey-Marie.

I, **Todd Gulich**, have a special offer for you, the reader of this chapter. Come to our shop and we will offer you a free $25 gift card towards you next oil change. Just call us at .... to start your Liberty Tire and Auto experience!

You can reach us at (248) 681-9710 or visit www.libertytac.com
We are located at 6485 Cooley Lake Road, Waterford, MI 48327

The Referral Miracle:
The Fable Of The Magical Coins
By Charles Gifford,
President, Local Business Network

Once upon a time in the land of Lessyfare, there lived a businessman named Horatio. Horatio was an honest, hard working businessman, but never seemed to be able to find true success. Then one morning, as he was reading the newspaper, an advertisement caught his eye. The headline read: FREE MAGICAL COINS.

The ad had been placed by a shopkeeper in the poorer section of town. Horatio read on. The ad claimed that the magical coins being offered were of absolutely no value to the person to whom they were originally given, but if that person passed them along to someone else, they would be of great value to that person, hundreds or perhaps even thousands of centars (the local currency).

Horatio was a kind hearted person, perhaps to a fault, and he thought, "Well, I'll be in that part of town today. I think I'll stop in and see what this is all about. If there is any truth to it, perhaps I can help some of my friends." Still, the advertisement's claims seemed a little hard to believe.

Later that day, Horatio was in the neighborhood of the shop listed in the ad and he stopped in to see what these magical coins were all about. The shopkeeper was a venerable old gentleman by the name of Charlemagne Giffard and he claimed that the ad was absolutely correct. Horatio could take as many coins as he wanted, but had to give them to someone else within 48 hours or they would lose their value. And the coin had to be given to an individual in the profession printed on the coin. As Horatio looked at the coins, he could see that each coin had a different profession printed on it – money lender, fisherman, carpenter, doctor, etc.

Still skeptical, Horatio took a dozen of the coins, selecting the professions of friends and relatives he knew would appreciate a little extra money. That day and the next he distributed the coins to his friends, explaining the claims that had been made.

The next day he began to get calls from his friends thanking him for the coins and telling him stories about customers who mysteriously appeared asking for the coins and then ordered hundreds and in some cases thousands of centars worth of products and services. Horatio's friends wanted to know exactly where Horatio got the coins, so they could get some and return the favor to Horatio.

Over the next week, seven or eight of Horatio's friends stopped in and dropped off a coin with Horatio's profession printed on it. And to his delight, seven or eight new customers stopped in, asked about the coins and ordered thousands of centars worth of merchandise.

Horatio didn't quite understand why it worked, but he knew a good thing when he saw it and went back to the shop for more coins. This time he took <u>two</u> dozen and distributed them all to his friends within 48 hours.

The results were the same and the money was beginning to pile up in Horatio's bank account. He returned to the shop again and took <u>three</u> dozen coins this time. He had noted however, that some of those to whom he had given coins had never returned the favor. So he either gave the coin to someone else in that profession or increased the number he gave to friends who had given coins back to him.

Life was beautiful. Everything was going great. Horatio's bank accounts were overflowing, his wallet was overflowing, and business was booming, because Horatio made sure that every new customer that came to him got the best of treatment and became a permanent customer.

BUT THEN, A TERRIBLE THING HAPPENED!!! Horatio woke up. It had all been a dream. Horatio was so disheartened, so depressed, because it had all seemed so real. But then, it occurred to Horatio that there was another way to make it all come true!

He gathered a group of his friends together, those who had brought the magical coins to him in his dream, and shared his idea.

"Why don't we work together to help each other. As we're talking to our customers and friends, why don't we look for opportunities to promote the other person's business? Every day I talk to people who need the

services of money lenders, carpenters, real estate agents, doctors, etceteras. When I hear someone say they need something one of you can provide, I will refer them to you. If you will do the same, we will all grow and prosper. After all, aren't referrals just like the magical coins in my dream!!

1. They cost nothing
2. They are of no value to the person who gathers them, but of great value to someone else.
3. If you give them to someone willing to give back, you are rewarded handsomely for your kindness.
4. The more you give, the more you get!

If we all learn how to generate referrals for each other, we will all become wealthy. From this day forward, I will dedicate myself to gathering referrals for each of you. I will gather as many as I can, because it costs me nothing, benefits you immensely, and will benefit me in the long run as you do the same for me. Sure, some of those to whom we give referrals will not give back, but that doesn't matter, because it costs us nothing and what we do receive in return will be worth thousands and thousands of centars."

Most of Horatio's friends agreed immediately that this was a great idea. Some were skeptical, but decided to give it a try. And some just couldn't grasp the concept and refused to participate. Over the next few years, Horatio and his friends worked hard at generating referrals for each other. Some were good at it and some were not and those that were not eventually dropped out of the group.

Those who grasped the concept grew wealthy beyond their wildest dreams and lived happily ever after.

THE END

There is a moral to this story

Referral networking involves the creation of personal wealth through the capture and exchange of information valuable to others. Your job is to learn how to capture as many referrals as you can and exchange them with fellow Local Business Network members, who are willing and able to do the same for you or others within LBN. Those who do not participate by bringing referrals should not expect to get referrals and will not prosper within LBN. But those who do will reap great rewards. The more referrals we all generate, the more we all prosper. Remember:

A referral costs nothing,
Gives great value to the person to whom it is given
Creates a desire to reciprocate within the recipient,
Is rewarded by referrals that will increase your personal wealth.
The more you give, the more you get!

We can all make our lives magical simply by helping each other!

About The Author

Charles Gifford is the President of Local Business Network and the co-author of "Network Your Way To $100,000 And Beyond" with Minesh Baxi. You can learn more about LBN at www.LocBusNet.com and benefit from 52 networking tips taken from Network Your Way to $100,000 and Beyond! at www.NetworkingSeries.com.

Seven Matchmaking Tips for Finding, Dating, and Keeping Business Referral Partners

By Gail Michelman and Louis Weiss

The art of building lasting *alliance networking* relationships is an art like dating and requires a strategic thinking approach to marketing. Through a Strategic Thinking Process (STP) our business group developed a marketing system to strategize, build, and acquire business allies that produce a constant large volume of referrals with more profitability.

Having studied over 100 books about networking survival, we have found that the science becomes a watered-down repetitive formula of follow-ups and phone calls. What is missing is "tie-ups" that have made major inroads in such industries as retailing, consumer markets, and particularly in financial markets.

A referral that you give out is really the act of putting your reputation on public display every time and requires a significant degree of risk. You need to find the right business ally whom you trust, who is credible, and someone whom you can become close to both personally and professionally. You can create "Ally Networks" through licensing agreements, joint-venture agreements, distribution-rights agreements, or more loosely in team-marketing relationships. When you are a small company, a strategic ally can allow you to piggyback your whole business onto the superior marketing and distribution structure of a well-established larger company.

Ask anyone about "business relationships" and you will likely hear descriptions that include trust, credibility, and profitability. Talk about referral networking and they will mostly describe it as a necessary evil, as activity that is more short term with varied results, and most of the time just not-working. But what if, beforehand, you could know where your referrals came from, what type they are, who is being referred, and you received referrals of the same quality almost all the time?

In its simplest form, *alliance networking* is the deliberate linking of two or more well-established company brands to establish a collaboration where their joint profitability and market exposure is greater than if the brands operated in isolation. Generally, each company involved with *alliance networking* will benefit more by working together.

Powerful synergies evolve from these business relationships that tend to be long-term, visible, credible, and more profitable. *Alliance networking* on average can increase your market share by 5% to 20% in the first year and can account for tremendous business growth. At most, we suggest that you maintain a limit to strategic allies for networking of five to eight companies so that you can improve the depth and intimacy of your group.

1. **Look for the perfect mate.** Start by dating your business associates to find out all you can about them. Do you remember dating—how we just needed to *find out everything* we could about the other person? We were always asking questions. Likewise in *alliance marketing,* the key is to find an *ally* that has the same values as you do. Look for offsetting skills that can propel your two companies together faster than apart. Many times you and your business can experience significant growth through an "*alliance networking team,*" which is a group of like-minded individuals collaborating on a marketing project.

2. ***Find "allies" with the same core target market.*** Complimentary industries are those industries that are directly satisfying the same customer's needs in similar ways. We know a successful team of real-estate professionals that got together after a severe market decline a few years ago. A client, a local realtor, was instructed to locate a mortgage lender, title person, appraiser, and a home repair individual. They rented a bus for property investors. They picked up the investors, who were looking for foreclosures, and brought them door-to-door, shopping for investment property. As a team they were able to solve their consumers' need better together than separately. Within one year's time, each of the team members had seen a 40% growth in business revenue. When a group of like-minded people collaborate on providing a customer-based solution, they will always be much more powerful together than apart. Also, a significant

amount of synergy happens from these power groups of coaching, accountability, creative marketing, and having in place a reliable system for cross-networking referrals.

Vertical markets, sometimes referred to as "pathways," are the direction that customers travel along the paths of their buying process.

Consider that the winter cold has ended and that you are ready to start your spring house cleaning. A pathway team may consist of a gutter cleaner, roof cleaner, window cleaner, and rug cleaner. The team creates a mutually beneficial advertising relationship where a local 800# takes the team's advertised inbound calls. As the spring-cleaning work progresses for that one customer, the word-of-mouth referral marketing from your ally group brings in the next team-member referral to earn and profit.

Alliance referral networkers must understand the products and services that are made available by each other in order to promote the team. The truth is that very few people deserve to be part of your alliance referral network. You must be selective because your main goal of an alliance partner is to qualify prospects and open doors to quality business opportunities.

3. *You may start getting marriage jitters.* Be sensitive to each others' needs and make sure with multiple allies that the relationship is equally balanced. At the beginning stages it may be a good idea to commit to paper a formal agreement. Make sure you have an exit strategy in case the relationship changes in the future. Talk about how you will resolve problems and issues as they arise. *Alliance networking* is about developing trust and long-lasting relationships. After learning more about each others' needs and exposing more networking opportunities, your relationship will deepen.

4. *Whose turn to do chores?* As with any relationship there is an amount of effort needed to have and to maintain. Who is responsible for certain activities? What was said last month during your meeting? Yes, being in an *alliance network is like being married.*
   • Follow a clearly defined execution framework.

- Have a preset group of marketing activities to generate a constant flow of quality referrals.
- Set a clear picture of the management functions, responsibilities, and a way to track your results.

Allies should update all interested parties of the progress of the *alliance networking* and the associated marketing activities on a quarterly basis, at a minimum.

5. *Fall in love with your marketplace.* *Alliance networking* gives you a dramatically faster way to grow and less costly marketing system by leveraging the word-of-mouth marketing of others. Alliance referring cannot be a one time affair. Get to know everything you can about the business and industry that you have selected. Keep yourself visible and people will think to refer you much more quickly if they have seen you in the last month.

6. *Respect and honor each other.* Networking is about seeing how we can help others. It is an art of giving and receiving.

Look at the business marketplace from your client's perspective.

- How is it that you can be a solution for them and make those ways the most effective way to promote your company?
- Is there any new idea to make it easier to find real-estate property for investors like a *foreclosure bus?*
- Isn't there a way that is less stressful to get good service to do my spring cleaning this year?

The process starts with market research: analyze your ideal customer, your competitors and your ability to serve these customers. Narrow your focus and target the best prospects that you want to reach and become the provider of choice.

7. *Surviving the long haul.* You must have a good offer that really motivates other businesses and their customers to try your business. Sometimes a free gift or percentage-off coupon can be used as a loss-leader incentive to bring in new business. Whatever you select, enjoy the alliance journey.

Have fun with the collaboration and there will be rewards. When networking roadblocks occur, use the synergy of your group to create answers to your situation. Success is being able to grow a profitable business that is fun, makes you happy, and makes others happy.

Using the idea of growing your business with *alliance networking* is a simple marketing system that brings in constant rewards for many years to come. This "tie-in" tactic quite simply is based on having Cross-networking partners and receiving word-of-mouth referrals.

Two additional bonus points:

Marriage can be a good thing. The beauty of *alliance networking* is that someone else tells people how wonderful you are and what you have done. Now you can know where your referrals come from, what type they are, who is being referred, and you receive constant referrals of the same caliber most the time. Get all this and more in rapid speed when social media networking is added to your chemistry.

In good times and bad. *Alliance networking* strategies can range from highly sophisticated agreements with financial investments to loose verbal handshakes. The main thing to bear in mind when approaching ally businesses is that you are giving them the chance to build their own profits, get more customers, and receive the praise of their customers for referring them to a quality business. For *alliance networking to work,* all parties must work closely together to create business. Follow the best practices, be patient, and manage the referral relationship closely and you will be rewarded with profits and respect into your silver and golden anniversary years.

> *"Profound, simple, and effective, I found Gail & Louis'*
> *Referral Networking system & Strategic Thinking Process*
> *(STP) to be truly a blueprint any business owner could*
> *follow when they are ready to deepen their relationships*
> *with key contacts and survive tough economic times.*

This is truly a roadmap to business success."
—JOHNNY "THE TRANSITION MAN" CAMPBELL,
DTM, AS Change & Generational Marketing Expert.

Speed Networking *is the greatest way for us to get more
exposure into our Non-Profit and increase our public
awareness. We put together a fund raising campaign
that literally replicates itself year after year. Our focused word-of-mouth networking we learned from their
consulting ideas accounts for 90% of our membership
donations annually.*
—MASTER CAPTAIN JEFFREY LOWN, President &
Founder of the Sport Fishing Foundation.
A television show producer "On the Fly",
and author of 9 published books.

About the Author:

Gail Michelman and Louis Weiss
Gail and Louis help companies who want to meet a lot of business
people and acquire a large volume of referrals. Louis is considered
the "Business Matchmaker." www.Mr-Alliance.com

**Would you like to be a leader of a 6-person Social Media and
networking group in your area?**
Email Gail and Louis at **SocialNetworking@comcast.net** for a
COMPLIMENTARY One-Year membership.

Gail and Louis have built a nationwide community of close six-
person teams that provide you with support, accountability, and your
own mastermind think tanks. The design is simple; you select your
own team members to meet every other week. Who should become
members? Any small business person that wants to increase the
exposure and receive more repeat business. Marketing together, you
have 600% more exposure than going it alone.

Who Do I Know Strategy.... Who You Want To Know & Why
By Natalie DeLeo

What do your clients get when they hire you? Obviously they get your world-class products and service, what else?

In today's competitive marketplace, not only should you be delivering beyond the clients' expectations, you must be able to become a great resource for your clients' needs.

What do I mean? In the next few pages, I will go over in detail how you can become a trusted advisor so your clients start to rely upon you as the gatekeeper to people that they can trust. You can maximize the relationship by educating your clients about the type of businesses that you feel comfortable in referring to them.

Before I lay out the game plan on how to go about creating your network and introducing the businesses within that network to your clients, let me share a little bit about my background.

After having played the role of a house-wife and mother, I was ready for a new career. Real estate attracted my attention and I chose to become a real estate agent. It was a lot of fun working with clients and helping them solve their problems. During this relationship, it became evident that I needed to refer my clients to other professionals who could help them. They needed services of people like a good loan officer, a landscaper, an appraiser, a furniture salesperson and so on.

This is when I developed my strategy that I call – Who do I know that you should know.

This strategy gives me dividends in two ways:
- First of all my clients are happy that they can get the best service they need without having to thumb through yellow pages and maybe make a mistake by hiring the wrong professional
- Secondly, my referral partners love getting referrals. They look at me with even more respect as a professional and give me referrals which prevents me from having to spend money on advertising

While I was working as a real estate agent, I referred a lot of business to one company for mortgage services. This company did a great job of taking care of my clients and I was so impressed that I left my real estate career and started working for them. This company is Mortgage Resource Plus, Inc. in Birmingham, MI.

What separated them from other companies were three things. I look for these three qualities in my referral partners too.

Here are those three key attributes:

1. A clear vision of core values

Do you or your company have clear core values? Without a doubt core values should be the base of any company. Our core values are reviewed with employees etched in our minds, in writing, and reinforced every chance we get. When we see a slip in communication all we do is go back to the core values and find which one we were lax in, learn from it and move on.

Let's take one of our core values at Mortgage Resource Plus- *Learn, Improve, Grow and Repeat.*

You must stay educated. Are you keeping up with all the changes? How much time are you spending on educating yourself and researching your client's needs? At least 2 hours a day would be devoted to staying abreast of the changes in your industry.

Learning from every transaction something new and sharing it with your colleagues is a big part of having a strong team structured business.

From what you have learned now you can improve your process to make the next client's experience even better.

If you do not grow from the learning and sharing you will become extinct. So decide what you have learned, what you improved upon, and how you can grow from it and then repeat it again & again

2. Candid -Open and honest communication

If you are a loan officer, do you communicate your turn times for the loan processes so that the client has a clear picture of how a loan gets approved? If there is a delay in the process do you tell the client right away or do you wait it out and stall the closing because you are afraid of them not understanding? Step up to the plate to deliver the good news along with the uncomfortable news.

Expectations of great communication should be upfront; verbal as well as in writing.

Do you communicate to the client how much you appreciate their help in getting documents to you on time and how much they have helped you? Do you send them a thank you for their help?

3. Be creative and consistent

Think out of the box. I've found the secret to success without cold calling and without spending hundreds and even thousands of dollars, on advertising. It is very simple, and I'd like to share it with you. You must have heard that – consistent mediocre marketing beats once in a while brilliant marketing.

I use different tools available in my industry to educate my clients consistently by email and mail. With numerous changes taking place in the market, I owe it to my clients to assist them in making better decisions. If you have a mortgage or even if you own a house free and clear, you are concerned about the market value of the house and also possibly, whether you are in the right mortgage product for your current situation.

So let me ask you, does your company possess these three qualities? I hope so.

I build strong, honest relationships by
- narrowing my focus toward making and sharing connections
- finding people who share the same business philosophy, that have their core values in place like I do
- knowing that these people have the same passion about their businesses

This allows me to refer people to those I trust, and to become a trusted referral partner in return.

Did you know the closing of a mortgage loan is one of the most stressful times for the borrower?

I attend all my closings and hence I demonstrate my trustworthiness and integrity, as well as the exceptional service I promised. Agents, Clients and Title Companies love it when I attend my closings.

Building Strategic Referral Partner Relationships

It was quite exciting that the people that I had known for those 3 years in the real estate business were now *my* strategic partners because they knew how I had a passion for great service and I knew they did too!

I thought if I already had a few great people I was receiving referrals *from* and giving referrals *to*, then what if I had *dozens* of people that thought the same way I did? I began to expand my business network of referral partners cautiously and systematically.

But as time went by, my thinking expanded and I thought, "what if my clients called me whenever they needed *any* service and if I had the right person to provide that service to them, then they would be so happy that they would want to refer me to all of their family and friends".

So I started listing all the people I had worked with successfully, and all the services I could imagine my clients would need during a home purchase or refinance such as:

Insurance agent

Tradesman i.e. plumber, carpenters, electrician, & painter.

Home inspector

Real estate attorney

Moving company

Cleaning service

With those thoughts my philosophy became, "Who do I know that you should know", and it has worked for me ever since.

The challenge was how to find more of these special people. I didn't want to go through the Yellow Pages. So I decided that in order to better please my clients, I would find out who they recommended. What better place to find great people but through your clients.

I started calling my great clients and asking them to help me. Everyone loves to help out and tell you about a great experience with a business person.

Then I asked my clients to introduce me to this person. First, I'd ask them if they would make the initial call to introduce me. They always say, "Sure I will." I would make the warm call to the perspective referral partner. The client calling first made my call easy then.

I'd like to share an important tip-- when I called and asked my client if they knew an insurance agent that they trusted and would refer to their family and friends, and they said, "No, I really don't right now."

Then I would say, "Well that's fine, thank you for your time. You know, in my search for an agent, when I do find a great one is it alright if I call you back and let you know who they are, so if you decide to switch agents you have someone that comes highly recommended"? Of course they say yes! It is a win-win situation for you and your client.

Power networking is another avenue of building strategic partners. This allows you to meet many more people and is sometimes easier to discover if they really think the same way you do. Done properly, networking can be addictive!

I joined a networking group called **Local Business Network** (www.locbusnet.com) back in 1999. This was a new venue for me. I was getting in front of people and getting to know people but some did not necessarily fit with my list of desired partners. I decided to join a networking group to meet more people I thought my clients needed. But it was upon meeting new business people, I was surprised to find out that my clients did need these types of services, and in turn these businesses' needed me! In my mind, I did not think that any of *my* clients would be asking for a website designer, but over the course of meetings and sitting one on one with this person, I found out that the type of client he had in mind was exactly the type of client I serve.

That was just the start. I met a new realtor, insurance agent, inspector, owner of a UPS Store that could handle my self employed people etc... Now I hit a gold mine! My list was growing and all because I wanted to meet people that thought the same way I did and that I could refer to my clients when they needed those services. And yes, every time I referred them, they would call and thank me and refer me in turn.

My clients directly benefit from the relationships I have developed along with the people from, *"Who Do I Know That You Should Know."*

Mortgage Resource Plus (MRP) has been unique from the start because they have never advertised, they simply help clients through business partnerships and clients with the purpose of providing a service that they want to refer. MRP has a passion of serving their clients & educating them. We work through options and use a mortgage as a smart tool to create financial freedom. We work hard to earn our clients and referral partners trust so we can help create a win-win solution for all the parties involved.

"Who Do I Know That You Should Know," is all about building a cohesive group of trusted alliances who help our clients get the best service they want and deserve. By building a network of referral partners, when our clients ask "Who is the best moving company?" or "Who should I call to get estimates on my roof?" We have the answer. We also have a large group of referral sources which allows me to focus on finding solutions that clients are seeking.

In summary, please do yourself a favor and re-examine how you have structured your business. Where do your clients come from and look at how many trusted relationships have you developed? Ask yourself, "If you were the client, would you be wowed by the service that was just provided and would you feel comfortable enough to refer your family & friends?"

If the answer is anything less than an absolutely YES then find the weakest link in your process and change it. Take great care of your referral partners and keep supporting their business. BE A GIVER always and you will never go wrong.

Speaking of giving, email me your address today and receive a "FREE CD." Each month I have different business building tips or interviews with top speakers.

It is not just the mortgage that Natalie can take care of; she plans on being your concierge for any need of yours, your family's, or friends and neighbors. Not only has she referred my moving company, she has included Changing Places Moving in seminars that she has held, and marketing pieces to her clients. She discreetly works her network of partners into her clients lives, leaving the transaction complete – completely PERFECT!

— JOHNNA GOODWIN, President,
Changing Places Moving (248) 674-3937

"It is clear to me that the team at "Mortgage Resource Plus" has a vision of devoting time & effort into building long lasting relationships with those whom they refer. The support they give to their referral partners exceeds those of many. Good work! Stay Focused."
— GINO WICKMAN, Creator of the Entrepreneurial Operating System and author of the award winning book. Traction

About the Author:

Natalie DeLeo can be reached through email address natalie@mrploan.com or call me at 248-642-4600.

When To Pop The Question? Timing The Close
By Minesh Baxi

Think of a guy who is eager to marry his sweetheart, the girl of his dreams! When should he pop the question? Should he pop the question on the first date? Or should he pop the question once he knows more about what she is looking for and whether it matches with his own dreams or not? You get the picture.

Selling is no different. Usually one of the most difficult tasks for a salesperson is to know when to go for the close.

With so many forms of closing techniques available, which one to choose is confusing to say the least. In this chapter, I want to outline a few simple ideas that will assist you in getting much better results than you have gotten so far.

Here are 6 simple steps in creating a process that will assist you in closing the sales.

1. Overcome Your Fears

The first challenge in closing is your own mindset. An excellent book written by George W. Dudley and Shannon L. Goodson is "***The Psychology of Sales Call Reluctance®***".

In this book, the two behavioral scientists mention that every salesperson has some fears in the area of prospecting and closing. In fact they call it "Sales Call Reluctance®". They strongly endorse the viewpoint that without overcoming these fears, salespeople are likely to find it hard to get new clients.

I assess prospective employees and sales professionals using their Sales Assessment Tool. It reveals quickly how debilitating the fear of prospecting and closing is. If it takes too much emotional energy, sales may not be the best career for this individual.

We are not talking about techniques here. No amount of closing techniques can overcome this problem as it is more emotional than intellectual. The simplest thing to do is to take this assessment and find out what you need to work on to improve your odds.

The three common traits I have seen of great closers are:

    a. Tremendous self-confidence in themselves

    b. Unwavering belief in the products and services they are selling

    c. A sense of urgency to get results

Without these traits, you might have to knock on too many doors before closing the sale.

Let me encourage you to create a positive mindset and rehearse in your mind, visualizing the sale as if it has already happened. Anytime you find that there is a negative thought which is impeding your progress, find a way to quickly snap out of it by taking an action – from snapping a rubber band on your wrist to jumping up and shouting – YES!

Foolish? Maybe; it works though.

2. 7 Ways To Be Recognized As The Expert

In the first chapter you read that there are three questions you must answer before a prospect buys from you. The questions are:

- Why should I buy the products or services you are selling?
- Why should I buy from YOU?
- Why should I buy NOW?

If you have answered the first two questions to some degree in advance then you are likely to face less resistance; and in fact, the prospect is quite often eager to do business with you.

Briefly, here are seven ways you can be established as an expert:

1. Becoming an author
2. Gaining media attention in newspapers, TV, Radio etc
3. Endorsed by a Celebrity
4. Client Results and testimonials; Referrals
5. Speaking in front of your target market, seminars
6. Member of a prestigious organization
7. Having a compelling web presence by having high ranking in the search engines and flattering articles and endorsements on numerous websites

    Bonus: Joint Ventures with Successful people

My personal focus has been on designing information products like audio CDs, DVDS and books which help educate the prospect while creating compelling reasons for the prospect to buy from me. In fact, Chuck Gifford and I broke down our book *"Network Your Way To $100,000 And Beyond"* into 52 video clips and articles that people can access at *www.NetworkingSeries.com*

Also you can receive for FREE, the audio CD "*7 Ways To Be Recognized As The Expert*" directly from minesh@mbaxi.com or at *www.NetworkingSeries.com*

3. Qualify, Close, Present

So you are ready to meet your prospect and you have prepared an excellent presentation. You have the power point slides or a brochure to show all the features and benefits of your wonderful products and services.

You can't wait to show your skills in telling all the aspects of your fantastic product.

This is where a sales person makes his first mistake. The most important rule in closing a sale is to ask more and talk less!

With a presentation in hand, are you likely to talk or listen? Very likely you will talk until the person is possibly bored or clearly impatient to get on to other things. What should you do then?

Here is a formula I was taught in a teleseminar from an Australian. He said that most people follow the formula:

Qualify, Present and then Close.

He told us that we should just change the formula to:

<u>Qualify, Close and then Present.</u>

If you are confused, I can understand. I was too. Challenge yourself by applying this new formula.

Instead of focusing on the presentation, focus on creating a list of questions which will help you make sure you are in front of the right prospect. The right prospect typically means that this person has theses <u>four</u> qualities:

• Need,
• Money

- Power to decide and
- A sense of urgency to solve the problem

If the person lacks any of these <u>four</u> attributes, you have nothing to show this person. Pack up and go back to your office.

With your list of questions, you can find out whether you are talking to a tire-kicker or you are talking to somebody who is likely to buy now.

Once you have done enough <u>qualifying</u>, act as if the person is ready to buy. Some people call it the ***assumptive close***. Your goal is to uncover the aspects of the product or service that interest them and get a commitment that if you have the right fit, what is the next step.

Your <u>presentation</u> will now focus on what the buyer wants and not on what you have prepared in advance. If they need to know only two features and benefits, why bore them with twenty?

4. Get The Prospect To Answer The Objections

Your presentation will uncover some objections that you failed to address up front. That happens to the best of us. Don't despair. This is not the time to panic.

Here are three simple guidelines in overcoming objections:

a. Give yourself time to come back with a response.
- Take a deep breath. Ask the person to repeat the objection or use phrases like – do you mean… etc.
- Most of us are not prepared to answer every objection just like that. Sometimes you may have to get back to the prospect.
- Getting too defensive is the sign of weakness and glibly trying to answer the objection does not help either.

b. Make sure the objection is really critical to be answered. Sometimes the prospect throws you a curve-ball and it has nothing to with the sale. Getting that clarification helps.

c. Now turn the question over to the prospect and find out how the prospect would like that objection handled. Most of the prospects will tell you instead of you having to figure it out.

Sounds too easy? It can be. You won't know until you try it.

5. Keep Your Eye On The Goal

Most salespeople get too caught up in the conversation and are not focused on the end goal – The Sale! Keep coming back to the main outcome you want. After all you are not planning to be a visitor or just a guest. Your job is to close the sale.

Sometimes you may not get the sale in the first step but at least you know whether it is worth following up or not.

Don't confuse building rapport with closing the sales.

If you don't have the check yet, you did not get the sale yet. Persevere.

6. Prevent Buyer's Remorse

Every buyer has buyer's remorse. So how do you overcome that? There are things to do before and after the sale to prevent that from happening.

Here are two ideas:

a. Don't rush through the sale. Some people may sign the paperwork just to get rid of you and then call to cancel the sale. Make sure you are answering the questions and that they are comfortable in making the decision. Let it be their decision so they feel that they closed themselves.

b. Secondly, call them back once you get back to your office. Thank them for their decision to do business with you and see if they have any questions that were unanswered during the appointment.

It is possible to have a process that you can rely upon to get you the results you want. Make it your own system and not based on a memorized routine.

Going back to the courting example, do you know when to kiss the girl? If you don't, you were not listening very well. If the date is going well and you have been checking the temperature consistently, you will know when to kiss and similarly when to pop the question.

About the Author:

Minesh Baxi is successful co-author of "*Network Your Way To $100,000 And Beyond*" and "*Stop Hiring Losers*". Minesh helps businesses create the competitive edge by becoming known as an expert by creating information products like Audio CDs, DVD and books along with web presence.

To get your free audio CD "*7 Ways To Be Recognized As The Expert*" call 877-968-2500 or email minesh@mbaxi.com

5 Keys To Match Your Business Goals To Your Website

By Steve Hyer

Everybody seems to have a website or at least plans to have one. The questions are: do you know why you want one and do you know how to achieve your business goals with your website?

My name is Steve Hyer and as the President of IGD Solutions, a web design and web application company, I have met numerous business owners and corporations who have a challenge in matching their business goals and their website.

Sometimes they spend money they don't need to and quite often the website does not help them further their business.

So for your benefit I have listed here five keys which will assist you in having a much better game plan for your website and related applications.

1. The first key to success in matching your business goals to your website and to ensure success is to properly evaluate why you want to have a website.

- Do you need a website just because everyone else seems to have one? Your competitors may have an advantage if they have an online presence and you do not.
- You may want to get more business and generate leads from your website having your website actually work for your company as part of your sales force.
- Your website may be a resource for your existing or previous customers allowing them to find information they need and to do business with you.

Start by looking at your business strategy and your marketing and sales strategy. It is very likely that your website and online strategy should be complementary in nature and integrate nicely with your business, marketing, and sales strategy. If you have a team of direct sales people working different territories, then the web presence needs to support that sales methodology.

If you are expecting cold leads from your website from Internet surfers, you will need to integrate your website into that business development strategy. Your sales process will dictate what role the website can and should play in developing new business. If your business is extremely local and most of your business is walk-in, the website may serve your existing customers and may not be a resource for new business. A web strategy can address both existing and new customers, but this should be a conscious decision in the planning process.

As you go through the planning process of working out what you want to try to accomplish online, make absolutely sure that you define what success means for this project. If new business is a goal of your website strategy, you need to know how much new business is a reasonable expectation and how much new business you should be satisfied with.

2. The second key to success is to understand how people use the Internet and how visitors will use your website. When a visitor ends up on your website, it needs to be immediately obvious who you are (what company is this website for) and what services you provide or what products you offer.

If the user cannot tell just by glancing at the home page of the website who you are and what you do, it is likely they will move on to a website that can answer those questions.

One thing that is often forgotten is that you need to tell the visitor what it is you want them to do next.

- Do you want them to browse your products and services to see if there is a good fit?
- Do you want them to take a self evaluation survey so you can give them an immediate online evaluation relating to one of your services?

There needs to be a clear and concise call to action that tells the visitor what you would like them to do next. Once the user has decided that your company can help them by providing a product or service that meets their needs, then they will want to find out if your company is reputable.

3. The third key to success is to create credibility online. Once the visitor has decided your company can help them, there is usually one more step before they pick up the phone or send you an email. The visitor wants to know if your company has been around, if they will continue to be around, and if you have expertise in delivering the products and services they are interested in.

Start out by including all of your contact information (Phone, Fax, Email, Physical Address, and any possible other way to contact you). Then include a history and profile of the company and include information about the owners and also about your community involvement. Include links to partner organizations and membership organizations. A company that is well networked and connected is more likely to be around for years to come. If you have a physical store or office, include a picture of it online.

The look and feel of your website is also something that helps to add or detract from your online credibility. If your website has mistakes on it and the design looks like it is ten years old, the customer may be left wondering if you will give them the same lack of attention that you have given your website. The website must definitely be an asset to your credibility and not a detractor.

4. Some websites may be setup in whole or in part to sell products online. If that is the case with your website, the fourth key to success is to develop an online selling strategy. Increasing business directly through the website can be a viable option to growing your company.

If you have just a few products, the simplicity of an order form may be appropriate, while if you want to sell dozens, hundreds, or thousands of products, a full blown database driven catalog and shopping cart system are most certainly necessary. You generally want to give the customers the option to search by category, manufacturer, price, keyword, or department. Make it easy for the customer to find the product they are looking for. Then make it easy for the customer to find out about your company so the user can conduct their credibility evaluation.

Finally, it has to be easy to go through the purchase or check out process with no surprises along the way. Sales tend to be abandoned when an unexpected shipping charge shows up through the process. Try to offer free shipping as much as possible and try to make the price stand alone with no extras along the way.

With eCommerce, it may be simple to create an online storefront if you have done the proper planning up front. What may not be simple is generating sales from that online store. You must do a thorough competitive analysis online before you even begin to develop your online store. Compare your prices to others online selling the same items. While you may enjoy some benefit to not being located physically near a competitor in the offline world, online geography often does not matter. Your pricing usually has to be in line with the competition in order to see sales online. You must also have a dynamite marketing strategy to unseat the incumbent competitors online.

5. Whether you are using eCommerce to sell online or your website is just providing credibility for your business, the fifth key to success is to evaluate, update, tweak, and change your website and your online strategy going forward. It is very unlikely, even with the best strategy and the best planning that you will set up a web presence and have it automatically just work. In almost every case, you will need to have a process in place by which you measure the results of your website and then make incremental improvements to it along the way. Looking at your website usage information to find out where your users are coming from, how they are finding you, and what they are doing on your pages are invaluable and absolutely necessary information.

If you have setup various calls to action within your website, but no one is navigating to those pages, you know you need to make some changes in the site structure to make it easier for people to end up on those pages. If your users are getting to the call to action pages, but not completing the action step, then you know you need to tweak what your action step is to try to get some additional responses. If you have one thousand people looking at a call to action page and only 2 people completed the action, with a little work on that call to action, just a 1% response rate could lead to 10 or more additional customers from the website traffic you already have.

In almost every case, when you are starting out trying to gain success from your online strategy, you will want to start simple. You do not need to accomplish every objective in your plan within the first iteration of your web presence. Take your objectives in manageable pieces and complete each one before moving on to the next step.

Success online is something that is more like a marathon and not so much like a sprint. Start out by defining your goals and developing a strategy to accomplish those goals. Define what success means within that process. Make some assumptions and plan out the first version of your online presence while always keeping in mind what is coming in the future and what direction you are headed. Monitor the results carefully in terms of contacts, business, and website usage information. The key is to use the available data to make educated future decisions about your online strategy that will lead to the results you are looking for on a long term basis.

About the Author

Steve Hyer is the President of IGD Solutions, a web design and application company. Steve was the President of the Clarkston Area Chamber of Commerce 2006-2007.

For the readers of this book, we will provide a no-cost, no-obligation report on your website including the Core Fundamental Strengths, Suggestions for Improvements, Online Cross-Industry Analysis and Comparison to your Competitors. Contact Steve at info@igdsolutinos.com or 248-625-0817 to get started today!

Building Your Business Brand Using Audio, Web Video and Automated Sales Funnels
By Ted Cantu

You Will Learn:
- The 9 Families of Search Engines and Why You Need To Be On Them
- Why Using Audio and Video On Your Site Closes More Sales
- How To Build Your Business Through The Power of Video
- How To Lock Down Your Niche Using Online Web Video

The Most Powerful Trends Influencing Your Customers Today

Today the face of online internet communications has changed dramatically. Now your potential prospects are searching the web and scoping you out before they call your office. They are gathering information about your company before they will commit to doing business with you. Prospects want to see testimonials, witness product demonstrations and even test drive your services before actually buying them. Today these technologies are easy to obtain and even easier to use and are absolutely necessary if you want your business to be super successful.

There are several key components to keep in mind as we market our products and services to consumers. This will affect how the prospect will interact with us and how we can leverage our time effectively using digital media.

It is no longer necessary to rely on cold calling, using scripts, and use interruption marketing methods to get our points across. Our new prospects are educated and have been pre-selected and also pre-screened before interacting with you. They have seen your media whether it is your web video commercials, web video interviews, web video testimonials, or have heard your audio podcasts.

Get On All 9 Families Of Search Engines

It is important to think beyond Google when it comes to the search engines. There are at least 9 different unique families of search engines that you need to be aware of. Each of these search engines are absolutely essential when it comes to building your online brand.

Traditional Search Engines – Google, Yahoo and MSN have been the old standbys when it comes to the search engine world. This is what people think of when search engines are mentioned.

Podcast Search Engines – Think Podomatic, Podscope, The Podcast Network, Get A Podcast.Com, and many, many more. These search engines carry audio podcasts and places them in the appropriate searchable categories.

Blog Search Engines – Technorati leads the parade when it comes to blog search engines. But there are many others including: BlogSearchEngine.Com, IceRocket, Weblog, Google Blog Search, and many more. At the time of this writing there are 7,950,000 blog search engines out there in the web universe.

Video Search Engines - There are **16,100,000** video search engines out there online. You only need to be on about 40 of them. From there your video clips will get picked up and distributed by other web sites and industry blogs. You can blast your clip out to the public with automation submission software but be careful because they will focus on too broad of a range. Your business could end up on, "Americas Funniest Dog Videos" or "Bikini Videos" and this will not serve you well when you are trying to look serious in front of your audience. Pick and choose your position carefully when you submit your video clips.

Social Bookmark Search Engines – Here is where the public votes for what they think is cool or significant! These search engines are based on the peoples vote for what matters most to them. There are 8,510,000 of these sites in existence and the number is growing. The members of these sites can vote on subject matter and organize them according to metatag keywords, subject matter and niche category. Examples of this include Digg, Delicious, and Furl.

Hubs – These are automated pages that hold your RSS syndicated content. Every time you make an update to your blogs the feeds get updated on your hub pages. This becomes very powerful. Your pages can attract a large following and this directly correlates to your search engine rankings. The two examples to keep in mind here are Orkut and Squidoo. You are well served to construct your own too – for examples on how to do this log onto: http://www.1seomichigan.com.

Article Search Engines – There is an art to submitting articles and you must do it the right way in order for your articles to grow virally. I suggest submitting them through a paid service so they can get distributed through a network of 500+ search engines. This is the best way to get your material seen and in front of the right niche categories. Use a submission service such as http://www.isnare.com.

Industry Portals – Everyone thinks of Google and Yahoo when it comes to search engines. But you would be surprised how many industry portals there are for just about every niche category. There are search engines for Doctors and Dentists. There are special niche directories for hobbyists and for contractors that live in your own state. Make sure you get familiar with these portals and get your sites listed on them. Not all of them are free but consider the amount of niche traffic you can attract from these alone. It is a worthy investment.

Micro Format Search Engines – This is just in its infancy but it is well worth getting involved with now. The early adapters are the ones who will cash in first. As I write this there are many new mini search engines popping up for iphones and hand held media. You will want to have a mini version of your site created especially for the hand held device audience in the very near future. You can find out more information about it here: http://kitchen.technorati.com/search

Wikis – This allows the users to contribute and modify content to your community based pages. You can build them on many different subjects and create solid communities. Many of these are free and they do tremendous things with your search engine rankings.

SEO – Breaking The Rules To Get What You Want

Search Engine Optimization has changed and the rules have been dramatically altered. Now the business owner has more control using

Web 2.0 software tools and this ultimately has a powerful impact over their search engine rankings.

It is no longer necessary to do standard Search Engine Optimization, (SEO) to get what you want. The practice of using traditional SEO techniques are very complicated to the, "Non-Techie". There are many steps that you must put in place in order to get listed and ranked into a search engine such as Google. You can wait as long as a couple of months, (the standard waiting list used to be 7 months) in order to get listed and ranked.
We have dramatically narrowed this focus down to just 4 hours.

Keep in mind that we were able to achieve these results by bending the rules. My team is constantly reworking success formulae to achieve fast results on the search engines and so far 4 hours has been the record. This has set the standard for what we do.

It is easy to get overwhelmed when looking at all of this new technology. I always tell people to pick 3 things that they like the best and to run with it. Once you find something that works you want to repeat it and create more links for yourself.

Here is how you check your popularity on Google:
1. Log onto www.Google.com
2. Type this into the search window, links www.yoursite.com
3. Look to the right to see how many links you have

Repeat this process until you have some solid stability on Google. Remember that I personally created 4,447 links on Google in just two months. I did this with just 25 videos and 30 articles. I knew where to submit these and I got phenomenal results in a very short amount of time.

I always tell people that they have to know what they want out of life before they submit their media. Remember that you are surrounded by what you create. You are able to connect to your dream client in a matter of just a few hours. So take time to craft your marketing message and also write down what kind of client you want to service. You will attract the type of clients you want most.

We are creating a "Pre Sales Funnel" and our videos are establishing credibility. I always encourage people to submit video testimonials when they upload their video content.

Monetizing your business

I constantly look for new ways to shorten the waiting time between the seller and the consumer. If I go the traditional SEO, (search engine optimization) route I could be waiting as much as 7 months to get my web site pages ranked and listed on Google. I could totally miss a market trend, a tech wave or a buying cycle. I think that is much too long to wait for results.

You are much better off building a series of web pages that covers all the territory that you want to sell in. For example if you have a product or service that you want to sell in every state then you need to build a page for each one. If you really want to lock this market down there are certain steps you need to follow to accomplish this goal.

Get a domain that reflects what you are selling and where. (Example, www.MichiganRealEstateSecrets.com, www.ChicagoRealEstateSecrets.com, and so on)

Create web pages that have information on each of your markets, niches and target audiences. Do not be cheap on this if you plan on making money on the web.

Take your recorded media clips, (audio and video) and place them on a separate page and drive people to see that page. These pages should be designed to "pre-sell" them on your goods and services. This will filter out any unworthy prospects.

You should not let the web site pages do all the work. You need to still get involved with people and invite them to look, preview and participate in the web site environments you create. I have found this to be ten times more effective than cold calling or waiting for word of mouth to take effect.

Getting involved and taking an active role in your marketing is key to your overall success. Pre-selling and pre-qualifying should be your first objective in getting the attention of new clients and online customers. This is incredibly powerful once you get involved.

To illustrate this point I want to address a recent situation in my own personal life. I created an online video to sell a product that I was developing and I wanted to test out my list. I invited only 78 people to come and check me out online. Out of that small amount 18 people purchased my new product. That is a 30% conversion. This would never happen in a direct response mailing campaign. These numbers are huge and the response was overwhelming.

I learned a considerable amount of information from my customers when I used pre-recorded media. I was able to adjust my selling approach and find out what my customers and prospects were searching for. It was critical to find out this type of information. I was able to gather their concerns and address them in a recorded format instead of getting on the phone and spending endless man hours explaining our products and services.

Here are the benefits:
1. We established credibility as an industry leader through pre-recorded media.
2. Unqualified candidates are easily identified – saving us the trouble and expense of meeting them face to face.
3. We are able to get our charts, graphs and testimonials seen by qualified prospects.
4. Cost effective. We are able to cut down our direct mail costs through the use of automated selling systems. We can use the same email list multiple times to get our prospects in front of our online presentations for literally pennies.

Working The Pre-Sell

Selling a $10,000 dollar item on the web may seem very difficult but there is an art to this transaction. I always found it was easier to sell a "welcome kit" at a low level amount, (ex: $250 - $487). This was the precursor to the larger ticket item. Selling a welcome kit to the customer ensures them that they will be well taken care of. There is a magical kind of psychology that works brilliantly here.

I prefer to have the online customer download a PDF order from off of my web site and fill it in with their credit card information. Then they can FAX it back to me and I will have their complete credit card on file. This is going to be very important when you start to work a continuity program, (go to my web site for more information on how this can work for your business... www.saynotoppc.com). If you rely on an online credit card transaction you will never gain access to the complete credit card information. You will only have access to the last four numbers, (Ex: XXXX-XXXX-XXXX- 5678).

You will want to get an online merchant account that will accept all of your transactions with no limitations. Many online merchant account gateways will put a freeze on your account once you start making real money, ($10,000 - $50,000 a week). There are many new online merchant accounts that understand rapid growth and overnight success in ecommerce. Check around to make sure that there are no limits to how much money you can make.

About The Author:

Ted Cantu is the president of i-Mobile Media. He is revolutionizing how business is done on the Web by connecting people through online automated selling systems. He has brought 35 different industries to the top of Google in a matter of hours through unrelenting innovation and perseverance. These are the techniques and strategies that will catapult you to the top of the search engines in a matter of hours.

FOR MORE INFORMATION: www.getyoursiteranked.com

PART THREE
Leadership and Management Makeover

Why Should You Be A Leader?
SUSAN WEST

Break Through YOUR Income Ceiling In 8 Simple Steps
Have An Amazing Team That Delivers Wonderful Results!!!
MARY DUNLAP

Don't Be The Gopher, Be The Executive
GARY PIPIA AND MINESH BAXI

15 Steps To Retaining Your Best Employees
T. VARATHA RAJAN

How To Make Sure Your Computer Consultant
Is An Asset To Your Company And Not A Liability!
DAN IZYDOREK

Why Should You Be A Leader?

BY SUSAN E. WEST

Why should anyone be a Leader? Let's begin by taking a look at the question "What is Leadership?"

Leadership is communicating to people their worth and potential so clearly that they come to see it in themselves, states Stephen R. Covey, The 8th Habit.

John C. Maxwell, author of Developing the Leader Within You says, *Leadership is influence.*

These are two of my favorite definitions of leadership. I would also add that leadership is a responsibility. You are responsible for how you influence others, to know the impact you have on others. If you are already in a position requiring leadership, you must have a greater awareness of what you say and what you do. Leaders are always being observed, analyzed and critiqued. So as a leader, do you know the impact you are making? Are you influencing people, communicating their worth, lifting them higher?

People move in and out of leadership roles all the time – as a parent, as a volunteer, as a project manager and as a VP, COO or Business Owner. Each one of us should be prepared to lead and be able to step into a leadership role when a situation demands it. I believe leadership is a journey, not a position or a title. Each one of us should be committed to leading in our own life.

So why should anyone want to be a leader?

There are five reasons. These five reasons can be remembered by the word *GIVES*. A leader gives – gives her knowledge, gives her time, gives her commitment.

Here are the five reasons why someone should want to be a leader:

G **Gain Awareness and Clarity About Yourself.** Learn your strengths, weaknesses, values and unique contribution

I **Increase Focus and Direction in Your Life.** Knowing where you are going and how you can contribute ultimately makes you happier

V **Value Others and Contribute to Others.** As a leader, you contribute to others growth and success and build their confidence.

E **Earn Respect and Reward**. As a leader you feel valued. And the numbers do not lie - leaders earn more money.

S **Set Goals and Achieve More**. There is great satisfaction in setting and achieving your goals.

Let's take a look at "G" – ***Gain Awareness and Clarity About Yourself.*** To be a powerful leader, you must become aware and recognize the impact of your leadership. It takes observation and inquiry to understand where you are today. You must begin to identify your strengths, what's working, what's not working and what's missing. There is a simple and yet very effective process that initiates the steps for uncovering your personal perceptions of yourself and the perceptions others have of you and your leadership. Learn more about yourself, confidence builds and you lead with greater ease.

Second, let's review "I" – ***Increase Focus and Direction in Your Life***. To be a passionate leader, you must have the ability to see clearly all that there is to see and be. Dreaming opens the imagination. Dreaming lets the creativity flow. Dreaming has no restraints. As a passionate and powerful leader you must find the time to dream.

It is out of your dreams that you create your personal vision, your specific purpose. Everyone is different. Take the time to dream about what you want to do, who you want to be, what you want to have. One of my favorite quotes is from Walt Disney, "All of our dreams can come true, if we have the courage to pursue them."

You cannot pursue what you cannot see. As a leader creating a picture, a dream and sharing that dream is what will pull people together, motivate them to action. A DREAM pulls you forward out of the murky day to day activities.

Third is "V" - ***Value Others and Contribute to Others***. This is a critical component of leadership. Being able to value others and contribute to others means you must be clear on what you value and what unique contributions you can give to others. You must define your own leadership values – clearly and uniquely; understanding what you hold in high regard and what drives your decisions.

Leadership involves making decisions. As you move up the leadership ladder with more responsibility and more people following you, the more value based decisions are required for you to make. Values are what are important to you. Core values cannot be compromised. These are the ones that show up when you are under pressure.

When we honor our own values, regularly and consistently, life is good. Life is fulfilling.

Interestingly, Elvis Presley said, "Values are like fingerprints. Nobody's are the same, but you leave 'em all over everything you do."

Fourth is "E" – *Earn Respect and Reward*. Earning respect as a leader comes from your interactions with others and results that you deliver. Leadership experts state "The organization is a reflection of the leader." Other experts have said, "You teach someone how to treat you by the interaction you have with others."

Take a moment to think about this. If the leader is always short with others, rushed, rescheduling or cancelling appointments, most likely you will find the balance of the organization doing the same. If the leader does not demonstrate value for her own time, then being accountable for the impact of how she and her team use their time is lost and not respected. Ralph Waldo Emerson once said, "Trust men and they will be true to you; treat them greatly and they will show themselves as great."

Becoming a powerful and passionate leader is an evolving process of different experiences, interfaces and results. There are moments of crystal clarity and befuddled mishaps in your day to day leadership experience. Both are necessary. Acknowledging your own growth allows you to better understand what others experience. Your ability to give thoughtfully to others in time, advice and feedback will earn you respect. Opportunities begin to open up for you to seek and grow as a leader.

Lastly, "S" – *Set Goals and Achieve More*. You must have a Leadership Plan. For all major projects at work, for all major goals at work, companies create a plan. As a leader, the leader of your life, you need to create your own leadership plan.

Having the Dreams defined, having the Vision clear, and knowing your Values is not enough. Establishing the next step, identifying the milestones and creating an overall project plan are the next step in aligning reality with the vision.

My request of you is to begin the process of unleashing your leadership power by making a commitment to yourself. ***Make a commitment to becoming a passionate empowered leader and be a leader that GIVES.***

Visit www.LeadershipPowerTips.com to discover how you can be a leader that GIVES.

About the Author

QuadWest Associates, led by Susan West, specializes in high performance leadership initiatives for executives, business owners and corporate managers. Building upon 25 years of business experience, QWA offers a comprehensive range of leadership programs, coaching and motivational speaking options that are individually tailored to each client's preferred style of learning, availability, and desired results.

Break Through YOUR Income Ceiling In 8 Simple Steps
Have An Amazing Team That Delivers Wonderful Results!!!
By Mary Dunlap

Do you feel that your practice has hit a ceiling?

Over the years you have developed a successful practice --- you are to be congratulated! BUT more paperwork, time and resources are being used to generate the same level of income or profit. Your income ceiling might have less to do with sales and more to do with leadership skills.

Let's find out what is halting your income and profit growth right now.

Ask yourself these questions ....
Part I
- Do two or more people on my team handle an issue or problem before it gets resolved?
- Do I have to be the one resolving the issue?
- How often am I the decision maker on procedural issues?
- How many times have I said "has anyone taken care of .....?" or "Where are we on .....?"
- Do I feel that I am the "only one who cares"?
- Do I consider my employees as an expense?

If you answered "yes", "too often" or "I am not sure" – then leadership may be the issue and not your sales skills

Part II
- Will I have someone remind me to take care of a business opportunity for next year? For something that happens 2 years from now? That will happen next week? Next month?
- Do I leverage my employees?
- Do I know much does it cost my business when I meet with a client?

- Do I know how much did it cost my business for servicing a client for the year – phone calls, issues, staff time, research, etc.?

If you say "no", "not always" or "I'm not sure" - then start to look at your employees as an investment resource and have them give you their passion and expertise.

Part III
- Would You Like to Have More Income & Profit While Working Less Hours and With Less Stress?
- Would You Like to Have More Income & Profit in a "Super-Charged, Positive" Team Environment?

Then This Chapter is For You!! I have worked with hundreds of clients to increase income and profit for their practices.

<u>Here are some problems you might be facing</u>
1. A firm can't understand why team members are not taking initiative and in fact are leaving. No one wants to change things or suggest better ways of doing things
2. A business owner feels that when she delegates work, it still comes back to her to finish. She gets frustrated because she does not understand why the person won't take the next step to finish the task.
3. Business owners feel that they miss opportunities because either they see the action item long after they should have done it or the client asks why this didn't get done.
4. Business owners feel that certain team members do not have the timely follow-through that is needed. The business owner feels that he has to remind everyone about everything.
5. Businesses price services and later find out that they are delivering more (which is good) but it is taking longer to deliver (which is bad) and it involves more people and steps (which can be worse)

What does this cost —— what you see

- Employees are leaving — this cost is easily 2 to 3 times their annual salary — lost time, training, clients and business opportunities.
- You are paying more for less
- Increased stress — affecting your and other's health
- Decreased production — lost opportunities and affecting the business' reputation

TAKE THESE 8 STEPS TO BREAK THROUGH YOUR INCOME (& PROFIT) CEILING!!

1. Your employees are your investment for now and the future
2. You are the leader – don't be just an employer
3. Decide what you want to be and where you want to go
4. Have your team and your clients decide how to get where you need to be
5. Don't reinvent the wheel and don't be a lunatic
6. Calculate risk versus reward
7. Let go and see what happens
8. Let's synchronize and meet back at 9:50

1. Your Employees Are Your Investment For Now And The Future

The first thing you need to do to break through your income (and profit) ceiling is to realize you can't do it all by yourself.

Many of you are already thinking "I already know this – I have employees."

For accounting and tax purposes — salary, professional development and incentive compensation are listed as expenses.

Do you consider it an expense?

OR

Do you view and act as this is an investment to take the practice further?

How to Act so that employees — team members are seen as an investment:

- Include team members – do things "with" them not "to" them. Team members are members not belongings.
- Determine how team members view you as leader. How they view their role and future in your practice.
  - Many organizations have surveys for employees that you can use to get an idea of their views. *(See end of chapter on how to get surveys)*
- Include team members in business meetings — strategy and implementation.
- Let them know what you want for the practice — the vision and mission

2 . You Are The Leader – Don't Be Just An Employer

You will find that team members will respond with passion and excitement <u>when they feel that you are serious about being the best leader.</u>

You really need to take a hard look at yourself! It's not what you see BUT what others perceive.

- Create a Strong Business Culture
- Set the example.
- Listen and be open to ideas from everyone. Reward for ideas that are used (have rewards for ideas used and reward again for ideas for their success).
- Encourage and Enhance Communication – regularly work to break down barriers to communication.
- Encourage team members to take risks and to grow.
- Build trust, cooperation, support and cohesiveness.

3. Decide What You Want To Be And Where You Want To Go

You need to determine and share your VISION and MISSION (with team members and clients)

VISION

- This is about the future – where the company will be; how the company wants to be perceived --- The vision statement is motivating, exciting!

MISSION

- This is about where the company is now, what the company is and what the company does and the quality with which the company does it.
- What we do each day – that will lead to fulfillment of the VISION
- This is a statement of PURPOSE -- it should inspire and excite.

4. Have Your Team And Your Clients Decide How To Get Where You Need To Be

- Include your team members as mentioned above in meeting and generating ideas.
- Establish a client advisory board and survey clients. Many organizations have sample surveys. *(See the end of the chapter for how to get this information)*

5. Don't Reinvent The Wheel and Don't Be A Lunatic

- You need to be open to new ideas.
- Negative Business Culture easily invades your company once you and your team members feel that "nothing will ever change".
- Being a lunatic or insane – means doing the same thing over and over and expecting different results.
- Seek out what already works and adapt it to your practice.
  - Decide exactly what you want to change.
  - Go to conferences and seminars (in-person, virtual, blogs) to find someone who is successfully doing what you want.
  - Establish a recurring activity in your calendar to contact this person.
  - Send gifts of thanks to people that help you with advice, example and time.

6. Calculate Risk Versus Reward

- This starts with defining the process – get every step written down.
  - For businesses – the processes can be:

- Client Acquisition – marketing, referral – lead follow-up
- New Client Process – generally what you do for clients who are new to the firm and the work that you do. Include time for surveying.
- Existing Client Process
- Business Operations – Service/Transactions, Business Planning, Human Resource

- That means consulting your team members to help write every step down.
  - Each team member calculates the time it takes to do the task.
  - Be realistic and add more time to activities that require contact and follow-up. Get an estimate and double it.
  - Use the time to ask team members to work with you on who has "ownership" of the task and what the results of the task should look like.
  - Take overhead expenses (less the salary, compensation, benefits, insurance for employees) and calculate per month, week or year – get an average for the particular process.
  - Take the salary, compensation, benefits and insurance for each employee and estimate a "fee" per person which includes a "buffer" for profit.
  - Apply these figures to each part of the process – total it for the "fee" for the process for each client.
- Now evaluate if the work you do justifies the expense – see what can be done more effectively and efficiently.

7. Let Go And See What Happens
- Processes are really under the control of your team members.
- Business Owners need to concentrate on what they do best – business building, business development, lead in strategies, work with clients and develop team members.
- **Once you have established in step # 6 – the tasks and results — have the team decide who will be responsible for monitoring and updating NOT for the success only.**

Everyone needs to depend on each other for team success. We need to have others help us to become more successful — sharing ideas and helping out.

8. Let's Synchronize And Meet Back At 9:50

- Let your team members go out and work the systems.
- Then let them come back in regular meetings to update everyone (including you) on the results.
- Develop your team members and yourself to ask for help.
  - Let's be very clear here – asking for help is not to be confused with giving up responsibility. BUT you need to AVOID negative reinforcement.
- Positive Communication & Reinforcement means an environment where team members can openly acknowledge what they did incorrectly and where the team (and you) can suggest ways to help and do things differently.
- Positive Comments for people who are moving from incorrect actions to correct ones. COMMENT as they are working toward the goals – where they are making small changes — this gives them motivation to do more.
- FEEDBACK for areas where team members are not changing what they are doing. Where they continue to work incorrectly, inefficiently or ineffectively. ASK them to work with you — what can you and they do to change?

These 8 simple steps can be part of your calendar and routine.

If you can't lead your team members to communicate freely, to take ownership, to care – then how will you acquire and service more clients? (The #1 Driver for Better Business Results)

You are leading your clients toward their goals and success — then take the 8 steps to lead yourself and your team members toward your business goals and success!

"Mary Dunlap Consulting has been a valued resource for helping us to understand who should be part of our practice as well as to implement staff workflow processes. WE have relied on her expertise to advise us on people that we want to consider being part of our team and how to help those who are part of our current team in self improvement. WE know she is truly committed to our success and that of our clients"
— EMOND, BERGER AND ASSOCIATES, *Financial Planners, Fairfax, Virginia*

About the Author:

Mary Dunlap Consulting is a Practice Management Firm dedicated to making our clients' practices successful and a great place to work. For over 10 years, we have increased business production and net income by double-digit percentage growth per year, increased employee retention, and demonstrated successful recruitment of the right person for the right job. We help our clients lead.

Obtain the materials for increasing your income and profit as mentioned in this chapter.
- Get the employee survey and process so you know how to get your employees' passion, excitement and initiative back.
- Get the information on client advisory councils so you know you are going in the right direction and to increase your success in pricing fees accurately and profitably.

Contact Mary Dunlap Consulting for a complimentary consultation and to get these materials free. Email:marydunlapconsulting@verizon.net and phone 877-563-0540.

Don't Be The Gopher, Be The Executive
By Gary Pipia with Minesh Baxi

Are you tired of being the "be all, do all" person for your business? Do you find yourself so tied up in doing the mundane tasks necessary for operating the business that you don't have the time to be the executive of the business?

One of the most crucial elements in being a successful entrepreneur is the ability to separate your responsibilities from being the gopher employee to learning to delegate as an owner and executive.

Successful businesses have defined organizational structures. They also have policies and procedures in place. I have learned the importance of having such a foundation in my business and it has helped me achieve much success. As the owner of an electrical company, I found out quickly that I could not handle every project and perform every task. By defining an organizational structure with proper policies and procedures, I have the ability to be the executive and spend time improving and increasing business. It is truly a wonderful feeling to be the executive and no longer be the gopher.

I'm sure that is good news to anyone reading this chapter who is burned out and exhausted from trying to do it all. Hold on for a second before you pick up the phone to place a classified advertisement for employees. As I stated previously it is important to have the proper structures in place. So let's start with the following;

Are you ready to be an employer?

Do you know when it is the right time to hire? What about who to hire? Do you have any ideas?

There are very few professionals who have an idea of when they should hire or who they should hire. In most cases, business owners and managers believe that anybody can help them and can be trained in no time! So let us find out if you are ready to hire . . .

So Are You Ready To Hire?

Assuming you are profitable enough to pay your new employee, you can start by asking yourself the following questions:

1. Do you know the best and highest value use of your time?
2. Do you have a clear vision of your organization/department?
3. Do you have a clear, visual plan of processes in the organization/department?
4. Are these processes assigned to specific employees?
5. Do you have detailed job description for each position?
6. Do you have a compensation structure that motivates your employees for best performance?
7. Do you have a proven system in place to attract the best employees?
8. Do you have a proven system to identify the best candidate among the applicants?
9. Do you have a 90-day plan to orient and train your new hire?
10. Do you have a performance evaluation system in place for your employees?

If you have answered "No" to any question, then I encourage you to <u>do the homework and prepare for the hiring process</u>. This work cannot be done by other people for you.

You might use a coach or a consultant to help you in any or all of these areas. The sooner you complete this task, the better it is for you and the employees on your team. In fact, my coach Minesh Baxi keeps reminding me of how valuable my time is and has helped me implement these ideas.

Worse than making a bad hire is hiring a quality person but not being able to retain the talent.

Here are seven ideas to follow through on the hiring process.
1. Let's expound on some of the questions, beginning with understanding the best and highest value of the use of your time. When we begin to measure our time in dollars we seem to get a

better understanding of just how valuable our time is. Imagine how insulted you'd feel if someone asked you to perform a job for them and offered you minimum wage.

Being an owner of your own business more than likely you would be highly offended that this person offered to pay you minimum wage. Wouldn't you be a little upset that someone thought your time was only worth that? Well, it is time to get upset with the tasks that you perform daily that could be performed by a minimum wage employee. This continues all the way up the organizational structure. It is imperative that you assess the tasks that you are performing and evaluate it against what you are truly worth.

2. After assessing your worth it is important to determine your staffing needs. Some people find it difficult to draft an organizational chart when they are used to performing all the tasks.

However, begin by listing everything that you do daily, weekly, and monthly and use that list to determine what can be done by others. From this list you can develop certain positions.

Start with an organizational structure that fits your organization, you can always add additional positions and restructure as your business expands. Make sure you have a clear plan as to the processes to be performed, and a detailed definition of the duties associated with each position.

3. It is very important to implement a compensation structure which acts as an incentive to motivate employees. With incentive based bonuses or pay for performance compensation, employees are continuously motivated to excel in their duties.

4. After you have all of your structures in place the next step is to implement a proven system to attract the best employees.
- Know exactly what you must have as well as the things you are willing to compromise on.
- Determine the best places to find the best employees.
  It might be a newspaper ad or word of mouth advertising or

some other method but it is necessary to find the source that works in finding the best employee.

- It is also important to know what process you will use to identify the best candidate out of the pool of applicants.

5. Having a ninety day training and orientation program will assist new employees in getting acclimated to your expectations and train them how to perform the duties according to your specifications.

Having structured training programs not only trains your employees how to meet your expectations in working for you, but also keeps the level of frustration down. Employees that are trained properly are easier to retain. Proper training eliminates new employee frustration which can dramatically affect productivity.

Failure to have the proper training techniques in place can result in losing very valuable employees and cause you to have a high rate of turnover. This can ultimately affect your time to focus on being the executive and not the gopher.

6. Making the commitment to implement proper programs to assist in hiring and retain the best employees is critical to the success of your business. Once you have put the systems in place they are there and can be updated and changed as needed to fit any changes you might implement in your growth and expansion.

Remember to lead by example. When your employees observe you following the policies and procedures and standing on your foundation for excellent customer service they will follow in your shoes. The old saying "do as I say and not as I do," is not applicable in a work environment. Rather take the lead to follow your business creed, and your employees will follow suit.

7. After you have your staffing in place the final step is to ensure you have a performance evaluation process. Giving employees regularly scheduled performance reviews also gives employees the proper understanding of the procedure as it relates to the intervals and expectations of performance reviews.

PART THREE: Leadership and Management Makeover

Setting a consistent timeline of every ninety days for performance evaluations allows ample time to accurately evaluate performances.

Understanding the importance of transitioning from gopher status and handling all the aspects of your business is a process and it may take time to implement all of the policies and procedures. However, gradual progress is better than no progress at all.

Make sure that you have a plan in place and work the plan. Your first employee will make a considerable difference in daily operations and will motivate you to continue to move forward in working towards the ultimate goal of transitioning from being a gopher to being an executive. You will notice a phenomenal difference and will have the time to devote to growing your business.

The essential key to the transition from being a gopher to being an executive is implementation of proper policies, procedures, and guidelines and adhering to them.

This will not only allow you to focus on the executive aspects of your business but will also lay the foundation for a smooth running successful company. So stop being the gopher and be the executive. It's possible!

> *"From the first phone contact through the handshake at the end of the installation day, everybody associated with your company not only did their job, they excelled at it."*-
> — MARK AND SANDRA P.

About the Authors:

Gary Pipia is founder and owner of Oak Electric Company, a full service residential and commercial electrical contracting company. With many years of experience Gary has gone from gopher to executive and is experiencing the fruits of his labor with a very successful business. Go to www.oakelectric.com for more information about Gary Pipia and Oak Electric.

Minesh Baxi is the co-author of "**Stop Hiring Losers**" and you can download first two chapters and his seminar on the topic for free at www.StopHiringLosers.com

15 Steps To Retaining Your Best Employees

By T. Varatha Rajan

Are you aware that an average American changes jobs seven times over the course of his life?

People change jobs for a number of reasons – looking for interesting work, appreciation for the work done, wanting to have the feeling of being part of an organization etc. Most of the employees are dissatisfied with their employer or manager and are looking for a dream job or company to work for. They feel that they are not being treated or compensated well.

On the other side of that coin most employers are looking for loyal and productive employees to build and/or grow, profitable businesses. Employers want the business to be as worry-free and trouble-free as possible. Employers are not satisfied with the employees' productivity. Employers can't rely on the employees – hard to find the loyalty anymore. Every employer is looking for the right employee.

The question becomes what is missing here?

How can we find and keep the right employees in our organizations? How can we have a great marriage between an employer and an employee? When an employer and an employee understand that they are on the same side, then each will prosper more. An employer and an employee should be interdependent - working as a team to achieve the common goal. It is critical to find and address the missing link of the relationship between an employer and an employee.

There are several answers to find and retain the best employees.

Being an employer in the Information Technology (IT) industry, it is extremely important that I hire and retain the best employees. In this chapter of "30 Day Total Business Makeover" we will review fifteen ways to hire and retain the best employees. Let's begin….

1. Find Good People: Finding good people boils down to a science - people are found, not changed. Someone said that "we don't teach our people to be nice, we simply hire nice people". The first step is to hire the right person who is the right fit for your organization.

2. Welcome New Staff: make the most out of new staff by first making them feel welcome. We have a tradition of having the farewell. We also need to celebrate the new member joining our family – like a new birth or marriage.

3. Give Clarity: Make sure that the employees have a clear understanding of what is expected from them. Ensure employees understand their roles and the importance of them. In most organizations, there are discrepancies between employees' understanding of their job duties and what is actually expected from them.

4. Have the Proper Attitude: We have to set the attitude and philosophy right. Clients and Customers are the source of our paycheck, understand them, serve them well, listen to them carefully, and deliver more than what we promise on time, every time. Instruct the employees to treat every customer as same as their favorite celebrity, hero or friend. Clarify that they don't get paid for the hour but for the value they bring to an hour. Show them how they can go up on the ladder by providing the best service. Teach them that the rewards in life will be determined by what they do, how well they do it, and the difficulty of replacing them. Make them think of themselves as a resource to our clients; an advisor, a counselor, a mentor and a friend.

5. Give Proper Training: Never leave the new employees to start the job without having the proper training. Give them training in small, regular doses rather than one long course. Set a standard for each employee to follow – clarify the definition of "high performance". Also preparing employees to effectively handle more than one type of project improves their employment security. Training truly is a win/win situation. With training, you add value to the individual; then the individual adds value to the company.

6. Help with Effectiveness: Too many employees spend more time planning how to get the job than how to become productive and successful in that job. As an employer, it is your responsibility to help them to achieve more, be productive and make them successful. The challenge is to find ways to ensure employees effectiveness.

7. Set Goals: The key is to set targets or goals. Set the Goal that is SMART – Specific, Measurable, Attainable, Realistic & Time sensitive. Work with them to identify what's in it for them. List the obstacles that stand between them and their goal, List the skills and knowledge required and where and how to find them, Develop a plan of action and set a deadline for achievement. Set the goals with them – write it down - break down the goals. Request the employees to go through it daily and never begin the day until it is finished on paper. Tell them exactly what do you want them to do and then get out of their way. If we go to work on our goals, our goals will go to work on us. If we go to work on our plan, our plan will go to work on us. Whatever good things we build end up building us.

8. Evaluate Often: "Inspect" to make sure that you're getting what you "expect." Tell the employees up front that you are going to let them know how they are doing. Give honest and sincere appreciation. Praise immediately. Be specific in telling them what they did right. Encourage them to do more the same. Don't praise workers for doing average or routine jobs. They can't get by with mediocre work. Keep in mind to praise the performer; criticize the performance. Be specific in telling what they did wrong. Tell them how you and the management feel about it. Let them know that you are honestly on their side and remind them how much you value them. Keep in mind that failure is an event, not a person.

9. Accept Responsibility: Who is wrong? What is wrong? It's not about right or wrong – It's how you react to and handle the problem. As an employer, we have to accept complete responsibility for understanding and for being understood. We have to teach employees the same thing to apply everywhere. Real power comes by empowering others! Always be positive and encourage others, and remember you are truly successful when you can extend a strong hand to someone who is reaching out or just trying to hang on.

10. Always Motivate: Motivation is motive in action. People, who feel great about themselves, produce great results. Different people are motivated in different ways. Find out what makes them tick, and what turns them off? Some of the ways to motivate them are; try to motivate through the use of voluntary social and sports activities, keep the number of supervisors to a minimum, encourage your staff to participate in decision-making, make time to stop and chat rather than simply greeting staff, always ask staff for their opinions about decisions that affect them, stretch people with goals that push them to perform better, create career paths, give financial rewards, but do not put a ceiling on incentives – it limits motivation. Everyone is interested in WIIFM [What's In It For Me]. Rewarding them will keep their motivation high.

a. **The Carrot:** The enticement of a reward gets them going. Just as a carrot hanging in front of horse gets him moving, the promise of a payoff gets most people moving. Build the vision during this stage.

b. **Milestones:** Smaller rewards for partial completion of a task. Encouraging comments keep them going.

c. **The Prize:** Reward at the end for accomplishing the task. Do more than you promise.

11. Be Friendly and Kind: The best way to make friends is to be friendly. You can start with a simple smile, a cheerful hello, or a word of encouragement. The secret is to create a friendly environment AND to train people to be friendly AND to be friendly all the time. Your friendliness and willingness to help is a direct proportion to your success. How friendly are you? How willing are you to help? When there is a problem, do you try to get rid of it or are you the person who solves it? Mother Teresa said: "Kind words can be short and easy to speak, but their echoes are truly endless". Use kind, inspiring words with a helpful intent and a gentle tone of voice, and you build better relationships and move up the success ladder more quickly and surely.

12. Build Relationships: Relationships are built on putting yourself in the other person's position. Try to imagine how others may feel. You can deal with them more effectively and get along with them far better. In the business world, relationships are an integral part of success and failure. Most people don't know that when Thomas Edison's laboratory and factory burned down, he was 67 years old and carried no insurance. Before the ashes were cold, Henry Ford handed Edison a check for $75,000 with the words "no interest" written on it.

13. Have Unshakable Character: Personality opens the door and helps you to win friends and influence people at least temporarily, but character keeps those friends and maintains that influence. Build your organization with a rock solid foundation. As Zig Ziglar says, "You can have everything in life you want if you will just help enough other people to get what they want" truly helps make living a joy.

14. Use All the Resources: To be the best you can be for others, first you must be the best you can be for yourself. This means attitude, discipline, and self-education. As Mr. Jim Rohn says, "You take care of yourself for me; I'll take care of me for you". Always think of CANI – Continuous And Never ending Improvement. Apart from your talents, list the natural gifts that each employee has, and determine how each gift can be used to promote or build the organization. Do not under use people – it causes them as much stress as overuse. Communicate with your employees about what is going on in the company – they feel better about themselves, the company and their job. Delegate responsibilities – make them accountable. Everyone has great potential. It is the employer's job to find out, bring it out and cultivate them. Become genuinely interested in them.

15. Listen… Ask… Deliver: Listening well is the most critical skills in life and in business. Listening without bias or distraction is the greatest value you can pay to another person. Show respect to their opinion. Ask more questions to understand deeper. Normally the complete truth will come after 3-4 questions deeper in the conversations. Understanding the unspoken words, reading the lines in between are one of the major challenges in conversation. Asking questions deeper will help to eliminate those challenges. Finally, deliver more than you promise – on time, every time.

In summary to take care of your employees – business – you should:

1. Understand that the employees and employers are on the same side
2. Find the right employee, celebrate and welcome them
3. Clarify the roles and responsibilities
4. Create the right attitude and mindset
5. Give proper training, tools and help them to be more creative and productive
6. Help employees be effective
7. Create SMART Goals and action plan to achieve them
8. Inspect frequently what you expect from them
9. Take complete responsibility
10. Find the motivational factor and make use of them to achieve more
11. Be friendly and kind with the employees
12. Build relationships with the employees
13. Have unshakable character

14. Use all the resources
15. Listen… Ask… Deliver

About the Author:

Varatha Rajan is the founder and CEO of IT Works International Inc. IT Works provides best temporary / permanent talents for their client's needs, up-to-date technological training for IT Professionals, provide technological support to their clients. IT Works is a trusted partner and a solution provider for professionals and corporations. Please visit www. itworksintl.com for more information.

How To Make Sure Your Computer Consultant Is An Asset To Your Company And Not A Liability!

By Dan Izydorek

The most common problem business owners have in finding a competent computer consultant they can trust is lack of knowledge. The majority of business owners are not up-to-date on the latest technology and how it works, and therefore are targets for dishonest or incompetent technicians.

The biggest concern you should have as a business owner is not being ripped off by a con artist; the person you most need to look out for is a ***well-meaning but incompetent*** consultant. This type of consultant is not always easy to spot. But with the knowledge outlined in this chapter, you will be able to weed through consultants vying for your business and choose the one who is going to provide you with the best advice and service.

Why It's So Important To Hire The Right Consultant

We live in a rushed world of business. In this kind of environment, every second counts and you can't afford to have computer problems or server crashes slowing you down. Business owners depend on their e-mail, databases, accounting software and other office applications to be fully operational every day. When these applications don't function properly, it can be frustrating and stressful and make you feel you're at the mercy of your consultant.

The wrong consultant can make things worse. Remember, he is tinkering around with your business' critical and confidential data. That's why it's so important for you to invest a little time NOW. This investment will eliminate a lot of frustration in the future.

10 Warning Signs That You Hired The Wrong Consultant

The consultant:

1. Becomes defensive or argumentative when you ask about project costs or completion dates, or when you question his recommendations.
2. Won't guarantee the work or your satisfaction.
3. Talks down to you, uses "geek speak," and makes you feel stupid when you ask questions.
4. Is consistently late or rushed, and misses deadlines without an explanation or apology.
5. Leaves your office a mess.
6. Uses high-pressure or scare tactics to get you to buy.
7. Doesn't explain your options for resolving a problem or completing a project.
8. Doesn't follow up after completing a project.
9. Never takes a proactive approach to supporting your network, and doesn't offer recommendations to help you secure your network, save money or improve your company's productivity.
10. Doesn't offer a preventive-maintenance or monitoring program to ensure that your network is protected from viruses, hackers, data loss, downtime or other problems

Three Reasons That Small-Business Owners End Up Paying For Mediocre Computer Support

If you're like most business owners, you've paid for computer support services that you weren't satisfied with. Maybe the person you hired didn't really know what he was doing. Even though there are many computer consultants to choose from, most business owners settle for mediocre computer consulting services for several reasons:

Reason #1: You know even less about how to find a competent computer consultant than you do about how to fix your own computer problems. Fortunately, you've invested the time to read this chapter, which will clarify exactly what you need to look for. Most business owners don't have this information and therefore make quick, uninformed decisions.

Reason #2: You believe your business is "too small" to need professional support. The reality is that small businesses are every bit as reliant on technology as large organizations. In most cases, you deal with the same issues but on a smaller scale. If you can't send and receive e-mail, get a virus, lose files, or if you experience a major system melt-down, your business communication is halted, billable time is lost, client projects get delayed, and deadlines are missed. Small or large, these types of issues can dramatically add to your stress and hurt your bottom line.

Reason #3: You believe you don't have time to look for another computer consultant. This is similar to saying you're too busy chopping wood to sharpen the axe. Here's the truth: It WILL take you more time to research your options and the computer consultants in your area. However, once you've done the work, you'll have a great consultant who will make your life easier over the long haul. A great computer consultant is worth his weight in gold, just like a great tax advisor, CPA or attorney.

10 Features You Should Demand From Your Computer Consultant: Don't Let Them Touch Your Network Until You've Confirmed These!

Now that you understand the importance of investing time into finding the right consultant, there are basic features that you should demand, such as insurance, qualifications and references. These features are black-and-white and can easily be proved.

Then there are other features that are just as important, but are more of a "gut feeling" determination you will have to make, such as how well the person communicates with you.

Feature #1: Qualifications and Experience
As mentioned earlier, much of the trouble you'll run into with

computer consultants is well-intentioned incompetence. There are many people claiming to be professional computer consultants who shouldn't be working on business networks. Maybe they don't have the right experience, they've only been doing this type of work for a short period, they don't have the right tools or training, or they don't know how to fix your specific problem. Whatever their shortcomings are, it won't turn out well for the business owner who hires them.

Obviously, the more experienced your consultant, the better your chances of getting the right repair done quickly. Junior technicians who offer cheaper prices can take two or three times as long to repair your network (costing you more in the final bill), and may not provide the right recommendations or repairs, which means additional problems and service bills down the road.

Not all networks are the same. Every business has a different mix of hardware, software and configurations.

The more networks a consultant supports, the more experienced they become with a variety of different hardware, software and network environments. Many junior technicians have only seen one or two different types of networks and therefore are extremely limited in their knowledge of what works and what doesn't.

How To Determine Your Consultant's Qualifications And Experience

So how do you know if a consultant is qualified? Ask him the following questions:

1. **How long have you been in business?** If he's only been in business for 1 or 2 years, be careful. Many one-man IT consultants are here today and gone tomorrow.

2. **Have you worked on my type of network or problem before?** You don't want to pay him to learn on your time. Ask for references.

3. **May I see your resume and the resumes of your technicians?** It is perfectly okay to request a resume or summary of qualifications for not only the consultant, but also his staff.

> **QUICK TIP:** If the company you hire has multiple technicians, make sure you know exactly which individual(s) will be assigned to your account. If possible, get assurance in writing that at least one senior-level consultant will be overseeing your network.

Feature #2: Client References

This seems obvious, but a lot of business owners skip this step. Ideally, you want to speak to other clients who have businesses similar to yours. Some of the questions you want to ask are:

- Did the consultant deliver on his promises?
- Did he stay on schedule and deliver on time or early?
- Was he responsive and easy to reach in emergencies?
- Did he bill accurately?
- Did he nickel-and-dime you over every little thing?
- Did he stay within the projected budget?
- Would you use him again? Why or why not?

If the consultant seems hesitant to provide you with references or, at a minimum, client testimonials, think carefully about hiring him.

Feature #3: Multiple Technicians

If the consultant doesn't have other technicians to back him up, you could be left hanging in an emergency. While one-consultant companies are often less expensive, you get what you pay for. He may be too busy running from one client to the next to do more than a quick fix or to give you the attention you deserve. If he goes on vacation, gets sick or simply becomes too busy, you could be out of luck.

The second reason you want to demand a "team" instead of an individual is because no one technician has infinite knowledge of every type of software, hardware and situation. If you have a team of professionals working together on your problem, you have a better chance of getting the job done right.

Feature #4: Availability and Fast Response Times

Nothing is more frustrating than having to wait on a consultant to show up when you have a problem. Before hiring someone, ask the following questions:

- **Do you have a system in place for responding to emergencies?**
- **How fast is your average response time to an emergency?**
- **Do you have a response time guarantee?**
- **Will my dedicated consultant have a backup consultant who is familiar with my account and network?**

Feature #5: All Promises in Writing

Four Things to Get in Writing:

1. **Payment terms**
2. **Deliverables** – Who does what and when?
3. **Work schedule and pace**
4. **Guarantees**

Any professional firm will be happy to put these items in writing prior to starting a project. If the consultant you're interviewing makes excuses, it could be a sign that he's not confident in his ability to deliver on his promises.

Feature #6: Insurance

- They should have worker's compensation insurance in case one of their technicians gets hurt at your office.
- They should also have general-business liability insurance. This will protect you in case they make a major mistake and destroy critical company files or equipment.

Feature #7: Understanding of Your Business

Technology should represent more than a bunch of computers networked together; it should be viewed as a strategic tool to build your productivity, your profits and your relationships with your customers.

Unless your computer consultant understands the nature of your business, he won't be able to recommend solutions that improve workflow and profits. He can be the most brilliant consultant in town, but if he doesn't understand your business you won't get the most from your technology investments.

Here are some questions to ask yourself to determine if your consultant is truly a business partner or just a "computer mechanic" applying Band Aids to your network. Does he:

- Dig to uncover the source of the problem or only look to fix the surface problem?
- Ask thoughtful questions to understand your business?
- Explain how his recommendations will improve your bottom line and speed production
- Proactively recommend solutions, or wait for you to ask?
- Follow up on his work to make sure you were satisfied?

Feature #8: A Professional

I've seen it occur over and over again. A business owner hires a consultant sight unseen. When he shows up at your office, he's dressed sloppily and looks unshaven or disheveled. You're almost embarrassed that he's there in your office.

At a minimum, the consultant you hire should have a neat, clean appearance. Remember, if he's in your office, he is a representation of you and your business. This is especially important if you have clients in your place of business.

Feature #9: Detailed Reporting and Invoices

Every invoice you receive should detail what work was done and why. This will avoid out-of-control or incorrect billing, as well as sticker shock at the end of the month.

Feature #10: Clear Communication

Aside from slow or poor response times, lack of communication is the single biggest source of frustration for business owners when dealing with a computer consultant. In most cases, your expectations are not met and you end up paying for incomplete work that you are not satisfied with.

Here are some ways to know if the consultant you are considering is a good communicator. Does he:

- Avoid using technical terms and acronyms you don't understand?
- Ask probing questions about how your business operates and how you use your computer network?
- Explain the reasons behind the recommendations he made?
- Offer alternative solutions to your problems and explain the pros and cons of each?
- Detail everything you've discussed in writing?
- Clearly explain how the work will be done and how he will approach and complete your project?
- Bring up the downside or potential problems with a particular solution as well as the upside?
- Provide frequent status updates to your project?
- Never miss deadlines without explanation or warning?

> *PC Miracles has been doing our IT work for years. We were very happy when PC Miracles released the "Effort Free IT Platinum" plan. We had been asking them to provide this type of service and we are very happy with how it's worked out. We are able to predict most of our IT costs for the year. With the "Effort Free IT - Platinum" plan we have also received faster response times to our issues. When we do have an issue, after business hours, they know about it before we do and they have a technician addressing the critical issues the very next morning. We have also seen a reduction in downtime since being on the "Effort Free IT - Platinum" plan.*
> — JULIE JOHNSON, Owner Acclaim Legal Services

CALL PC Miracles for a FREE Network Evaluation to see how your network stacks up. Talk to Dan to hear how you can avoid the pitfalls he talked about in this chapter. PC Miracles usually charges $297 for this service but, as a reader of this book, it's yours free so call today or, for more information about this service, go to www.pcmiracles.com/EffortFreeIT/NetworkEvaluationOffer. When

PC Miracles' trained technicians come to do your evaluation, you'll receive a FREE Stainless Steel Insulated Cup, while supplies last.

About the author:

Dan Izydorek founded PC Miracles in 1994 to provide exceptional IT service support to small to medium sized businesses.

We have grown 15% - 30% every year. And still continue to service some of our original customers.

You can reach Dan by e-mail at Dan@pcmiracles.com or call him at 248-620-2201. PC Miracles' website is www.pcmiracles.com.

PART FOUR
Financial and Risk Prevention Makeover

Use Your CPA To Give Yourself Peace Of Mind
MARIE A. JAKUBIAK, CPA

The 3-Step Financial Makeover
TODD RAMMLER. CMA, MSA

Maximize The Benefits of Your Business
And Minimize Your Exposure
ERIC GOULD, JD, LLM (TAXATION)

Your Free Cup Of Coffee, A Gas Card And 3 Questions
You Must Ask Before Buying Insurance
SHARON BARNES

The HSA: An Innovative Yet Simple Method,
Guaranteed To Reduce Your Personal Health Care Cost
KEITH PARKE

Why Your Father's Retirement Plan Won't Work For You
SANDRA WRIGHT WITH MINESH BAXI

A Contingency Plan – The "Do Or Die" Safety Net For Business Owners
PAT BYRD

What's The Enemy: Spending More Or Spending Less On Employee Benefits
TED HIMELHOCH AND MARTYN DICKINSON

BONUS SECTION:
Makeover Success Stories from Chambers/Associations

Use Your CPA To Give Yourself Peace Of Mind
By Marie A. Jakubiak CPA

Working with your CPA should be an enjoyable and satisfying experience – a win-win situation. Money is a powerful, yet stressful part of our everyday lives. Your CPA should be your partner in achieving your dreams and goals making sure you avoid the pitfalls of having money and not using it to make more money.

Why do you need a CPA?

1. You should never need to worry about the IRS contacting you and questioning your tax return. You want to rely on the expertise of a CPA to handle these situations.
2. You need to avoid "sticker shock" by planning and understanding what you are going to owe.
3. You need to review and understand your financial situation evaluating the best way to handle opportunities. You and your CPA should take a pro-active approach to making the right decisions for your overall financial situation rather than react to what you've already done.
4. You should use your internal financial information to evaluate and improve the profitability of your business. Your CPA should work with you to identify where your business can make more money.
5. Your CPA needs to be a true partner, being accessible to you and available when needed

1. The CPA and the IRS

When you go to the mailbox and find a letter from the IRS, most of us have physical reactions (knot in stomach, lump in throat) even before the envelope is opened.

By using an experienced CPA, your concern over what is inside the envelope is lessened.

CPAs have experience in speaking with the IRS and identifying what needs to be done to resolve tax issues. The CPA removes the emotion from the situation. My clients know that sending the tax correspondence to me results in an explanation to them of what is needed to comply with the request. I also make sure they understand what happened.

Sometimes, <u>but not always</u>, there is a piece of information that is needed and the issue is easily resolved. At other times, there is a need to pay money -- but a CPA is aware of options such as installment agreements and offers in compromise to address any balances that might require time to pay.

Your CPA should be experienced in working with the IRS to handle the issues.

2. Avoiding "Sticker Shock" – let's plan ahead

What is "sticker shock" for you? Is it not knowing that you owe large amounts in taxes? What about not knowing something was due to be filed with a taxing agency? What about not knowing critical bills remains unpaid? By planning ahead, any of these "sticker shocks" can be eliminated.

Tax compliance:

Business owners are overwhelmed with all the forms and returns that need to be addressed. There are surveys, property tax reports, annual filings and employee payroll tax returns due very frequently. A good CPA will keep track of all the little things that need to be completed to keep your business current. In addition to your annual income tax returns, they will advise you of due dates and the need to complete any necessary filing of forms for the various other types of taxes or assessments you may be subject to.

We all get plenty of information that we look at and (by habit) set aside. Certain of those "form letters" are important. A good CPA will advise you whether to put the form in the trash or assist you in completing it so it doesn't negatively impact your business.

Mid year planning and review to anticipate the balance of the tax due

Probably the number one complaint I receive from new clients -- they were given a huge tax bill at March or April 15th and didn't have any idea it was coming. When this happens, I ask how often the CPA reviewed the numbers with the owner and often they indicate that they didn't know their financial results until the return was done.

Both the CPA and the business owner should have at minimum, an annual tax planning strategy session. This review can be done at any time during the year and will depend on the size and needs of the client. If there is significant business growth, the business may want to plan every quarter. If there is little change from the previous year, a review near the middle of the 4th quarter may be sufficient. You, as the business owner, and the CPA, as the advisor should be checking the "pulse" of your business results and anticipating what monies you will need.

Why pay the taxing authorities any more than you have to before you have to? You need to anticipate what you will owe at the due date to make this happen.

Cash flow issues

The phone is ringing off the hook and you can't handle the sales orders that are coming in because you have to deal with creditors looking for payment. Tough times happen and require some quick and rational thinking.

Your CPA can project your cash flow and use some common sense financial analysis to determine who you need to pay first. Using computerized software often gives you reports which will assist you in projecting cash flow. The system can also "stage" your vendor payables to summarize the smaller vendors (those which may require a small amount of cash and take a large amount of your time) so that they can be paid off and reduce phone calls. Your CPA can also assist you in developing quick worksheets if the software formats aren't readily available.

Collection of accounts receivable is also a task that must be a routine part of your business. You may be financially successful but you need to be following up with customers to get payments in. They may not be running their business as efficiently as you. You could get caught with a bad debt if you don't follow-up and make sure they get payment to you.

If either side of the equation, cash coming in from accounts receivable or cash going out for accounts payable results in a shortfall, the focus needs to be placed on that area to avoid cash issues that can strangle your operations.

3. The proactive approach versus reactive approach

The repetitive nature of most businesses doesn't require a phone call to your CPA daily. Your CPA is a partner for you to call on when a "special transaction" such as a large transaction of business requiring some price concessions or financing arises. Speaking to your CPA will provide you with a more in depth analysis to determine if the decisions you are making are in your best interest. CPAs have several clients and the experience to look objectively at the impact on your business.

Once you've completed the transaction, the only action available at that point is a reaction. What if the situation results in a higher taxation? Did you determine the right price? If the job requires overtime to complete, have you taken into account the premium wages and other premium overhead costs? Your CPA is experienced in looking at this and taking those additional items into consideration. Keep them aware of "special transaction" situations. Having an objective outside opinion by someone who is partnering with you to achieve what's in your best interest is important.

4. Use your financial information to make more money

How can you make decisions about your business if you don't understand the changes occurring within your business? What would happen if your sales were to double or reduced to half?

Your CPA can assist you in determining what information you should review; however, the following list is somewhat generic to most industries.

• In what areas have your expenses changed significantly from year to year? Do you know why they increased or decreased? Was there a problem that needs to be addressed or can the differences be explained?

- Analyze your expenses as a percentage of sales? Why didn't the costs increase proportionately with your sales? Did you have increased costs that weren't reflected in pricing adjustments? Can you identify them and make the adjustments needed?

- Can you generate your profitability by profit line? Are you focusing your business on your most profitable business lines? Focus your business on the most profitable work you do.

- Do you know what your breakeven point is? Have you looked at your overall overhead? Is there any overhead that is variable based on your targeted sales volumes? What is your fixed overhead – (what it costs you even when you don't produce your product or service)? When times are tough economically, do you know where you can cut your expenses quickly?

- What types of employee benefit options do you have? Are there any other plans that might be more cost effective? Would a flexible benefit plan be more advantageous? Do you have the option of continuing with the existing plans but shifting some of the cost to the employee?

- Do you have a budget? Have you designated certain individuals as responsible for making the budget numbers happen? When budget numbers aren't being met, you can make adjustments improve the bottom line elsewhere even when sales aren't happening if you have the right monitoring procedures in place.

- Key ratios, such as inventory turnovers, days in accounts receivable, current ratios, and others are used by banks to make decisions about you when lending money. (Definitions of these key ratios (and others) are easily found on my website). Understand how these ratios may impact you should you have a loan with a bank and these ratios are covenants within the loan documents.

Specialized industries may require additional key points to consider. These points are more generic for service and manufacturing companies.

Do you have the right CPA?

Your CPA needs to answer your phone calls and respond with answers to your questions in a fashion that you understand. If they talk technical lingo and you don't understand it, you don't have a partner concerned with your needs.

Your CPA should help you remove stress from dealing with your money. They should provide you confidence that they are looking out for what is best for you. CPAs look for the long-term client relationship. You should too. It's always easier to open up about your big problems (and often money is one of them) to someone you've been through a lot of little problems with. Make your CPA someone who is on your side......helping you make more money.

> *"When we had problems with our balance sheet, Marie was able to identify the issue quickly and put our minds at ease. She is an honest and hard working person and has always been available to us. I would encourage anyone who is in need of CPA services to work with Marie.*
> — RENEE SIEGEL, Tri-County Floor Covering, Inc.

About the Author:

Marie A. Jakubiak is the founder of Marie A. Jakubiak & Associates, P.C. a certified public accounting practice in Bingham Farms, Michigan. Marie has over 27 years of experience. She graduated from Michigan State University, B.A. Accounting.

Marie is a member of the American Institute of CPAs (AICPA), Michigan Association of CPAs (MACPA) and an ambassador with the Rochester Regional Chamber of Commerce. Marie performs Peer Reviews under the MACPA-CART review program and is a Certified Quickbooks Pro Advisor. Visit the website www.majapc.com or phone 248-594-3034 for more information.

Book an appointment and obtain the CD "*10 things you can still do before year end to save taxes*".

The 3 Step Financial Makeover

TODD RAMMLER, CMA, MSA

"The Small-Business CFO"

It was around 7:30 p.m. on a Wednesday evening in April when my cell phone rang. It was Matt, a business owner I had talked to a few times at networking events around town. He was concerned. Earlier in the day he attended a quarterly financial review with his banker, and the banker did not react well to Matt's financial statements.

"The banker was asking all these questions, and I didn't know the answers. I'm an engineer, not an accountant!" Matt said.

Matt's company hit a bump in the road, and had lost money during the previous 15 months. But what concerned the banker were not necessarily the losses, but the lack of understanding as to what was causing the losses and what was being done to correct the situation.

Two months later, Matt's company was being pushed out of the bank.

At that point Matt asked for my assistance with this situation. When I first looked at Matt's financial statements, I wasn't surprised at the banker's reaction. The statements were a mess. There were errors, conflicting reports and omissions.

We spent some time reconfiguring Matt's financial statements, creating a consistent month-end process, training Matt and his staff on these changes, and implementing cost cutting strategies. We put tools in place to track performance and set objectives for the end of the year.

In 3 months, Matt went from a $300,000 loss to breakeven. By the end of the year, he made a modest profit.

The next year he experienced record profitability. Six months into the current year, he's already exceeded his profit from all of last year.

Welcome to extreme makeover, finance edition!

Important Note: This chapter is not about the usual financial topics – tax strategies, financing alternatives, how to hire a CPA, etc.

This chapter is about making money. Specifically, it's about using the data you have to make better decisions . . . to make more money. It's a rare glimpse into the thought process of an experienced CFO.

My firm provides outsourced CFO (Chief Financial Officer) and Controller services to small-businesses. In this chapter, I will outline the process we go through when we accept a new client—and the same process we went through with Matt's business. The specifics may vary from client to client, but the overall process is the same. Our objective is simple: use the data to maximize profitability. We follow a proven 3 Step Process. Here's an overview:

> **The 3 Step Financial Makeover Process:**
> **Step #1:** Organize the past
> **Step #2:** Understand the present
> **Step #3:** Create the future

Let's get started. . .

Step #1: Organize the Past — Format Financial Reports to make analysis EASY

It is impossible to make effective business decisions if your data is not organized properly. I've been a professional accountant, Controller, Finance Director, CFO for 15 years. My main focus has always been financial analysis – not tax returns, not audits, not GAAP (Generally Accepted Accounting Principles) compliance, not treasury – just financial statement analysis.

I'm continually amazed at the financial reports business owners use to make decisions. When I meet a prospective client, I ask to see their existing internal financial statements. In most cases they produce a document that is 3-5 pages long (per statement) showing current period information and possibly year-to-date or prior year data as well. I look at it and I see a bunch of numbers. But they're not organized in a fashion that is telling me anything.

Look, accounting is complicated. Debits, credits, GAAP, tax, accruals, reserves—it's enough to make your head spin. Unfortunately, it has to be complicated. But our objective is to take this complicated mess of numbers and organize them so that they create a picture. For the average business owner, it's like a puzzle that just fell on the floor – pieces everywhere, and just the thought of trying to sort it all out is overwhelming. However, if we build the financial reports properly, those pieces come together to create a picture that communicates a clear message.

I am a big believer in the KISS principle (Keep It Simple, Stupid). I'd like to share with you two of my KISS principles regarding financial statements:

KISS Principle #1: **If your financial statement cannot fit on one page, it's too long.**

No exceptions. Now if you want to use an 11 x 17 paper, that's up to you. But I have a strict one-page limit.

KISS Principle #2: **If I can't understand your financial statements, you can't either.**

By "understand", I mean being able to quickly find problems, see relationships, and draw meaningful conclusions.

After a prospective client has shown me their internal financial statements, I then show them a sample set of our *TRENDSPOTTER* financial statements laid out the way I would do it for them.

They all switch to this format.

Now, I could attempt to explain to you the specifics of how we put together financial statements, but as the saying goes, a picture is worth a thousand words. At the end of this chapter there are instructions on how you can get a copy of sample TRENDSPOTTER financial statements that are organized for analysis. This will provide you with an excellent starting point.

Some additional tips for creating financial statements that allow you to do analysis like a pro:

- Segregate different types of revenue into 2-4 main categories
- Segregate major direct costs (labor, material, subcontractors) into these same categories. These costs will be considered "variable" costs. There should be a fairly predictable relationship between these costs and the corresponding revenue line (e.g., labor is expected to be X% of sales, etc.)
- Create logical subgroups in order to condense the statement into 1 page. For example: rent, utilities, property taxes, trash removal can all be grouped on a line item called "Facilities Costs". If more detail is needed we go to other reports; but let's start with the 500 ft view, looking at the forest, not the trees.
- Similarly, don't show line items that contain minutia. Group any oddball costs together under "Miscellaneous" or some such appropriate heading. If you're a $5M dollar business, you don't need to see $50 for postage as a separate line item on your P&L. It's not relevant.
- Eliminate clutter – No pennies, no dollar signs.
- Create "dashboards" for the handful of items that are the keys to driving your profitability, cash management, etc.

Step #2: Understand the present — What is the data telling you?

"Financial analysis" is a boring, overused, vague term that can send people running for their pillow & blanket. But in the context of running a business, it is one of the most important things to understand, assuming you want to maximize profitability.

The objective of financial analysis is to understand what the data is saying, and make effective business decisions that maximize profitability, minimize risk, and protect company assets.

In laymen's terms, it means using the data to make more money.

To accomplish this, we begin with the one-page, TRENDSPOTTER financial statements described earlier. Using this type of statement we can tell if the key relationships for your business are out of line, and investigate those items further. Problems will jump off the page, such as:

- Costs posted to the wrong period

- Costs that have been missed (not posted)
- Cost posted to the wrong accounts (mis-posted)
- Jobs/Projects/Products whose margins are eroding, increasing, or contain errors.

We can also use this type of report to make important decisions relating to:
- Price increases
- Cost cutting
- Expansion
- Elimination of certain products or services

We'll be able to quickly calculate the breakeven sales level, or the amount of sales needed to generate 5, 10 or 15% profit. We'll be able to predict profitability for any given level of sales.

As you progress through the analysis step of the makeover process, it is quite common to have different systems or different components within the same system giving you conflicting information.

Financial analysis helps us find these types of issues and fix them. All your numbers, reports, and management information should be in harmony providing you with a clear and consistent message. Unfortunately, this is frequently not the case. Lacking the proper expertise internally, many business owners choose to ignore it and "hope everything works out" by the end of the month/quarter/year.

But hope is not a business strategy.

There is no substitute for accurate financial analysis.

Step #3: Create the Future – Projections become Reality

If you've ever listened to Zig Ziglar discuss goal setting – or done any homework on it at all – you know this: Goals that get written down are much more likely to be achieved.

If it is common knowledge that writing down goals is the proven, accepted way to achieve them, why not create written financial projections?

<u>Four Lame Excuses for not having written financial projections:</u>
1. We've always wanted to do it, but just haven't gotten around to it
2. We don't really know how
3. Our sales are unpredictable, so it's a waste of time
4. We've managed to get by for 10/20/30 years without them, so why start now?

Note that these are excuses that the average business owner would not tolerate from an employee. Try to imagine this conversation:

> **Business Owner:** *"Jack, I need you to put together a timeline for the ABC project to see if we'll meet the timing and budget requirements."*

> **Jack:** *"Boss, we've managed to get by for 20 years without a timeline, so why start now?"*

> **Business Owner:** *"Jack. . . . you're fired."*

Look, it is human nature to procrastinate, to avoid tasks that we're not sure how to do, and to get caught in "That's the way we've always done it" thinking. And I know business owners are busy and are constantly pulled in many different directions. <u>But this is important!</u> If you don't have the time or knowledge, find someone who does and get it done.

Projections do not need to be precise to be useful. Doug Hicks, author of *"ABC for Small and Mid-Size Businesses"* and an expert in financial modeling and Activity Based Costing puts it this way: "It's better to be *approximately* right than *precisely* wrong."

The objective is to put together a projection based on our best estimates and refine the estimates as new and better information becomes available. That way we've created a target, and we can make adjustments in order to hit the target – or change the target – or both. But without the target, we're playing blind archery.

If we have the projections in place and they are kept up, we can see future problems as well as opportunities that are coming at us, and make decisions on how to react to those problems or opportunities. Just because you've been successful for 30 years without projections doesn't mean you shouldn't do them. Things change. Ask anyone who's a supplier to the auto industry. What may have worked 30 years ago, will not necessarily work today. Furthermore, I can make a strong case that choosing to ignore this discipline is almost certain to result in leaving money on the table.

The 3 Step Process I've just taken you through is intended to bring clarity to the past, a tighter focus on the present, and visibility for the future.

If you have competent help, and can implement the 3 Step Financial Makeover outlined in this chapter you should be well on your way to achieving the 30 Day Total Business Makeover, and realizing the profitability goals you've set for your business.

About The Author:

Todd Rammler, CMA, MSA is the President of Michigan CFO Associates, a leading provider of outsourced CFO and Controller services to privately held businesses.

For more information please visit www.michiganCFO.com or call (586) 675-7605.

To get a copy of the whitepaper The #1 Financial Mistake Made by Small-Business Owners, please visitwww.michiganCFO.com/ freereport.

To receive sample TRENDSPOTTER financial statement layouts, send an email to info@michiganCFO.com and type "TRENDSPOTTER" on the subject line.

Maximize The Benefits Of Your Business And Minimize Your Exposure

Eric J. Gould, JD, LLM (Taxation)

The advice and guidance provided throughout this book should assist the reader to properly establish the business, develop a plan for success, and execute the plan. Once the business' foundation has been established, the next level of planning should be maximizing the benefits of the business while protecting the owner's wealth and assets from the claims of others.

While there are no "sure things", there are various methods for a business owner to create additional wealth and protect that wealth.

1. Strategy 1 — Insure the business' timely payment of taxes.

While this appears to be a common sense best practice, it is remarkable how many business owners fail to pay the government first. All taxing authorities charge penalties and interest for late payment of taxes, as authorized by law. The government is an expensive source of credit.

While a corporation and limited liability company shield the owner from the claims of the business' creditors, this protection does not eliminate personal liability to the government for unpaid taxes. The government has a vested interest in collection of taxes and the law does not permit an owner to just walk away from the company's unpaid tax liability.

Many taxes are held in trust for the government, as the business is a collection agent of various taxes, such as sales tax, excise tax, withheld income tax, and withheld social security tax. Section 6672 of the Internal Revenue Code authorizes the collection of all unpaid "trust fund" taxes from the responsible officers of a business. A responsible officer is generally any person who has the authority to pay taxes and chooses to pay other creditors (including themselves) instead of the government.

Many state laws hold responsible officers personally liable for all business taxes, not just the "trust fund" taxes. Many cities impose personal liability for city income and withholding taxes, and some laws provide that failure to pay over these taxes constitutes a crime. The message to business owners is clear – if the company fails to pay the tax due, the government will seek payment from the individuals involved.

2. Strategy 2 – Protected savings for the future. After insuring the taxes are paid, most successful entrepreneurs make sure that they save for themselves, by putting money away for the future. Retirement savings plans allow employees to save for the future by contributing money to a qualified plan. A key advantage to these plans is that the contributions are made using pre-tax dollars. The contributions are determined solely by the employee and deducted from salary before income and social security taxes are determined. Some plans permit the employer to make voluntary contributions, which are deductible. These are often referred to as profit-sharing contributions. Other plans obligate the employer to contribute money into a plan to pay for benefits in the future. These payments are generally based upon employee participation in the plan, such as "matching" contributions.

The funds contributed to these plans are for the benefit of the employees. The funds are placed in a trust, segregated from the business' and owner's personal accounts, and invested for future growth. The funds in the plan are legally protected from the claims of creditors, both of the business and the participants.

There are several different plan types and an owner must evaluate which plan will best meet the needs of the business and its specific situation. Retirement plans are subject to numerous rules and regulations, including contribution limits. Accordingly it is essential to consult with the business' professional advisors to determine the plan that is most efficient and appropriate under the circumstances.

3. Strategy 3 – Risk management with life insurance. Life insurance is an important part of a business owner's financial plan. Many owners look to the company to pay for life insurance.

However, most insurance premiums paid by the company are not deductible. Those looking to shift the cost of the insurance to the business should evaluate a split dollar insurance arrangement. This arrangement may allow the owner to obtain life insurance at a lower cost than would otherwise be possible.

A split dollar insurance arrangement is a written plan that in essence "splits" the premium payments, the cash value of the policy, the ownership of the policy, and the death benefits. The company pays the policy premiums. Receipt of life insurance coverage is an economic benefit considered compensation and subject to income tax. The amount of income included is based on a published table or rates or the insurance company's published rate for a one-year term insurance policy. These rates are less than the premium actually paid. An alternative approach is to have the owner pay at least a portion of the premium with the funds coming from taxable compensation, which is deductible by the company.

The policy proceeds will eventually be split between the company and the employee. Upon death or redemption of the policy, the company will be repaid the cost of insurance premiums paid and the employee or employee's beneficiary will receive the balance of the proceeds. It should be noted that some arrangements provide the company may receive the greater of the cost of premiums paid or the policy cash value.

A split dollar agreement can be an important business planning tool to achieve certain goals, including the retention of key employees. It must however be integrated with the overall plan and objectives of the business and the owner. Consideration must be given to the company's ability to fund this arrangement and the insurability of the owner or key employee.

4. Strategy 4 – Asset leasing. Consideration should be given to creating separate entities to own assets used by the company and have these entities lease the assets to the company. With a properly structured lease agreement, the lease payments will be deductible by the company. The rental revenue may result in income to the leasing entity, depending on the leasing entity's expenses. The leasing entity provides another source of potential income to the business owner.

Since the company does not hold legal title to these assets, the company does not risk losing the leased assets to satisfy any claims of its creditors. A creditor can only pursue the assets actually owned by the company it has a claim against. With proper planning, written agreements, and filings, the leasing entity may take preference or priority in the event of competing claims of creditors. This creates a further barrier to a creditor pursuing claims, as even if the creditor prevails in establishing its claim, the creditor may stand behind the leasing entity and other secured creditors.

It should be noted that the law provides creditors several protections against improper transfers and transfers to defraud creditors. An improper transfer could subject the business owner to personal liability, eliminating the anticipated benefits of establishing a corporation or limited liability company. Accordingly great caution should be exercised. Implementation of this strategy must be coordinated with the company's and the owner's existing obligations, especially with lenders who have an existing security interest. The leasing entity may have to subordinate, or lower the priority of, its position to an existing secured lender. It is essential that all leasing arrangements be properly planned, structured, and documented for this strategy to succeed.

The challenges and risks of a business are ongoing. A sound, firm foundation establishes a business, creating rewards for the owner. Once the foundation is set, the company can continue to grow and evolve. In this growth and evolution, there are opportunities to expand the rewards a business provides in a cost effective manner while minimizing some of the risks, both to the company and the business owner. A successful business owner will have a trusted and reliable "advisory board" to guide him or her along the way. Aside from the payment of taxes, the strategies above require input and analysis from an attorney, accountant, and financial advisor as to which strategy, if any, is most appropriate for the business and its owner to achieve the planned goals and objectives.

About the Author:

Eric J. Gould, Esq. is a shareholder with the law firm of Couzens, Lansky, Fealk, Ellis, Roeder, & Lazar, P.C., a full-service law firm with offices in Farmington Hills and Detroit, Michigan. He received a BBA with distinction from the University of Michigan Ross School of Business. After his law degree from Wayne State University Law School, he received a master of laws in taxation from the University of Florida Levin College of Law. He provides counsel and advice for tax planning, commercial transactions (including medical and dental practices), real estate transactions, general corporate matters, business succession planning, estate planning, and asset protection planning. He also represents businesses and individuals in tax controversy matters before the Internal Revenue Service and state and local taxing authorities.

Your Free Cup Of Coffee, A Gas Card And
3 Questions You Must Ask Before Buying Insurance
By Sharon Barnes

Most salespeople have one common complaint. Maybe you have said this to yourself – "I do not have enough appointments."

This is the biggest challenge in sales. Salespeople have memorized their presentation and they feel that they provide the best product or service to their clients but how do you get in front of the prospects? And on top of that, qualified ones?

Before I talk about the ways to get in front of prospects, let me take a short detour to help you understand the importance of focus in sales and how this can assist you in tackling the weakness in your selling. I learned from Minesh Baxi that a prospect has three questions before he or she decides to buy from you, the salesperson. They are:

a. Why should I buy the products or services you are selling?

b. Why should I buy them from YOU?

c. Why should I buy NOW?

Unless you answer these three questions satisfactorily, nobody is ready to do business with you.

The second point I want to make is that salespeople can get quite busy. They are running off to networking meetings, meeting different people, answering information requests from clients and prospects, mailing out pamphlets, designing better websites, etc. The bottom line is that there are only a limited number of activities that a salesperson can invest his or her time in. The only real productive use of the time, in my humble opinion, is in having face-to-face appointments with qualified prospects. Everything else is noise and distraction in building a successful selling career.

It is possible that your business revolves around doing business over the phone. In your case, the face-to-face appointments can be replaced with one-on-one phone calls with the qualified prospects. At the end of the day, how do you track your progress? If you did not have enough appointments, then you wasted your time away. Does this sound too strong? I hope not.

So you ask "How do you find face-to-face appointments with qualified prospects"? The bottom line is that you need to get out there in front of people. Some will qualify and some will not. But you will never know which ones qualify if you don't meet them at all.

I suggest a number of things for getting out there and meeting people: networking groups, being an active member of the local chamber of commerce, going to charity events and social functions, participating in associations, or any other function where there will be a number of people attending. If the person you meet is not in need of your services at that time then many times someone else they know may be. The key is to get out there and make a name for yourself!

I will buy you a cup of coffee and a gas card

My business is selling insurance. The moment I say that I sell insurance, quite a few people literally think I have plague! I know I am half-joking but the reality is that most people do not look at an insurance salesperson with deep respect and it is not like buying a new car or a home that you cannot wait to go see it.

So what are my choices? My focus needs to be on finding a way to get people to sit down with me and understand the needs of a good insurance policy.

Have you ever filed a claim and got burned? It is possible that you did not have the right coverage or the company was not a reputable one. Anything can happen.

So when should you find out whether your insurance policy will deliver or not?

Obviously before you need it! Right now you may be thinking, I am not sure whether I have the right coverage or not.

Excellent, in the next few sentences I will try to do my best to educate you.

But let me ask you, wouldn't it be better if I could actually sit down with you and go over the policy with you. That is why if you are in the vicinity of Oakland County in Michigan, feel free to give me a call and I will make sure that you get completely educated about your policy now before it is too late. I will buy you a cup of coffee and give you a gas card as well.

Today you must make it compelling for your prospect to take the time to meet with you.

What are you doing to make it worth your prospect's time to meet with you?

Timeshare resorts offer free tickets to amusement parks and overnight stays in attractive areas to entice you to meet with them.

Why? They know that they have qualified their prospects and they are well aware of their closing ratios. Do your homework to find out how many meetings will end up in actual closed transaction or a paying client. A term you must understand and apply in making such decisions is the life-time value of a client. How long do you keep a client and how much money directly will the client bring to you over this period? Clients who bring referrals can have a much higher life-time value.

Three Questions You Must Ask Before Buying Insurance

If you are like everybody else, insurance is something you look at as a necessary evil. While we are on the topic of insurance, you must ask these three questions before you pick your insurance:

1. Does the policy give me the coverage that I absolutely need for my circumstances?
2. Is the company reputable enough that it will help complete my claims quickly without giving me the run-around?
3. Is this the best price for the coverage?

Recently one of my clients was researching buying home insurance. I mentioned a few policies to him and these policies had obviously a range of premiums to be paid.

Looking at the premiums, he asked a little confused, "Sharon, why shouldn't I buy insurance from the company with the lowest premium?"

Has that occurred to you as well? In some cases the company with the lowest premiums does not settle claims quickly. You may have to wait for three to six months to settle the claim.

Despite knowing that the claim settlement could be an arduous process, some people still prefer the lowest premium hoping that they will never have to file for a claim!

I know you are smarter than that.

Here are some additional tips to help you make the right decision.

Unfortunately when it comes to purchasing insurance coverage a lot of agents have a "Buyer Beware" attitude. In order to make sure you don't get burned, adhere to the following rules.

When shopping for Auto insurance make sure these three points are taken into consideration before purchasing the policy:

1. Shopping for the Lowest Price Available: You get what you pay for so compare not only price but policy features as well. Not all insurance companies offer enhanced benefits so assess all the benefits included to see the true value you will receive.

2. Choosing Inadequate Liability Coverage: Liability insurance helps protect you and your assets if you cause an injury to other people or damage their property with your vehicle. If you choose lower liability limits (i.e. $20,000/$40,000), an accident that causes serious injury can result in medical bills and lost wages that could far exceed your minimum coverage and can potentially leave you financially exposed. It is recommended to purchase liability at $100,000/$300,000 or higher.

3. Evaluate the need for "Extra's" added on the policy. Many agents will add additional coverage without the client's full understanding that they are paying for those so called "extra's". These may include glass breakage, rental car, towing, etc. that are added onto the policy many times for an additional charge. Determine if the need exists before agreeing to them and keep in mind that often you will only receive a portion of money refunded to you instead of the total cost that you spent to rent a car or have one towed.

When it comes to homeowners insurance, don't even think about purchasing the policy unless it includes the following 3 items:

1. Include Water Backup of Sewer: Too many times I've heard of people calling their agent to report a claim that their sewer or drain has backed up, causing thousands of dollars of damage, only to find out that it is not covered. For a minimal price, this rider can be added and you will never need to worry again.

2. Purchase "Guaranteed Replacement" Coverage: Many companies say they guarantee replacement costs only to find out that when it comes time to collect on the claim, the replacement falls short of what is needed. Guaranteed Replacement (or sometimes called Replacement Cost Plus) can pay up to an additional 25 percent of the home coverage limit if there is a total loss of your home and additional money is needed to rebuild.

3. Scheduled Personal Property: Provides additional homeowners insurance coverage for high value items such as jewelry, watches, antiques and fine art. Without scheduling, all your items are lumped together with one coverage limit (and a lower one for Fire and Theft) and many times it will not actually cover the cost of your items.

If this sounds too much to grasp in one chapter, just call me and I can educate you either over the phone or by meeting face to face.

About the Author:

Sharon Barnes is an independent insurance agent and can be reached at (248) 207-5741 or by email at savvyinsurance4u@hotmail.com. She will buy you a cup of coffee and give you a gas card as well.

The HSA: An Innovative Yet Simple Method, Guaranteed To Reduce Your Personal Health Care Costs

By Keith Parke

Look out, world. The Health Care Revolution has already taken place. It has not waited for a new president to take office. It has not waited for the dire effects of global warming to melt the polar ice caps. It is not dependent on a government-mandated National Health Care Plan. The revolution I speak of has infiltrated the United States in the form of HSAs (Health Savings Account qualified plans).

HSA in Client's Best Interest

I was among the first healthcare benefit advisors to see the advantages of HSAs, and immediately I began to offer them to my clients when they first became available. Most "broker agents" refused to offer such plans because they were not in the "Agent's Best Interest." Obviously, lower premiums result in lower commissions so, as you might imagine, a lot of misinformation and confusion has been presented in the market place to discourage their purchase. Nonetheless, over 4 million Americans have enrolled in HSAs since their inception.

Initially, the insurance companies highly touted HSAs as the greatest thing since baked bread. Now that they have been on the market for several years many insurance companies are discouraging agents from selling them and instead are promoting traditional co-pay plans with lower individual deductibles yet higher out of pocket cost. Why? Because HSAs are not as profitable as expected. The insurance companies have found it very expensive to cover all of your medical cost 100% including prescriptions and routine doctor visits after you reach your deductible. Now think about that. If a product is not actuarially profitable for the insurance company, is it then keeping more money in your pocket? Obviously it is time to sit up and take notice of the HSA's ability to save consumers money in terms of management of healthcare costs. My goal in this chapter is to correct the resulting public deception and show the utility of the HSA plans.

Some Definitions: Premiums, Deductible, OOP, HSA

What is an HSA compatible plan? Simply put, there are two parts to it:
#1: The health insurance.
#2: Your HSA account.

#1: The HSA compatible insurance plan is a government legislated, high deductible (the amount you are responsible for) plan that offers little coverage until your deductible is met. After that threshold has been reached, the HSA covers at your choice of either 100% coverage (preferred) or some type of co-insurance such as 80/20 to a maximum limit. All family members' claims apply to one common deductible. Once your out-of-pocket (OOP) limit is met, most insurance companies now cover medical expenses including doctor visits and prescriptions 100%. **You pay $0.**

#2: The HSA account is an optional, separate bank account, used solely for medical payments. It can be funded by yourself, your employer or a combination of both. With a family plan, you can place anywhere from $1 to $5950 per year with no restrictions on how much (or little) money can go in at a time. The account is very flexible. The money placed in the account is pre-tax. It grows with interest, tax deferred. The money rolls over year to year and is never lost if you don't use it. It is designed to cover your medical needs. However, any money left over can act similar to an investment type account (like a 401K or IRA).

For those concerned about higher deductible amounts, simply take the money saved with lower premiums (your monthly insurance bill), and deposit it into the HSA account. When the amount equals your deductible you have created a $0 deductible health care plan, and **You keep the money** in the account (minus any claims) instead of the insurance company. Solid protection, lower cost.

In Summary there is Solid Protection when the two are combined:

HSA Compatible Insurance:
- Lower cost premiums.
- One Deductible (for the whole family.)
- 100% coverage (preferred) or co-insurance option.
- Full coverage after known OOP limit is met.

HSA Account:
- Pre-tax fund contributions
- Tax deferred interest
- Rolls over year to year
- Account funds cover Deductible expenses

Rock Solid Protection/No Surprises

Historical Note

As healthcare insurance consumers, most of us have been weaned on traditional, benefit rich, low deductible, low co-pay plans or HMOs (Health Maintenance Organizations, not to be confused with actual Insurance Programs). Consequently, having a plan that offers little coverage until you have met a deductible is not a warm and fuzzy feeling when you have a small claim. The comfort comes from knowing you are fully protected for the big claims

Historically, traditional plans exploded in popularity when unions fought for control in the manufacturing and automotive industries. Recent daily newspaper articles lament how these old plans have driven up health care costs and financially crippled the manufacturing industries that offer them. Prior to that period, health insurance was typically in the form of a catastrophic, hospital-only coverage plan. When you visited with your doctor (often in your home), you were responsible for the cost (often paid with a chicken in each hand). HSAs bring us back closer to this concept by making the consumer responsible for the little things yet eliminating the financial risk for catastrophic health occurrences.

Two Things Every Client Wants

I am about to introduce techniques which will lower your health insurance premiums. Ah, but you have heard this before. Anybody can lower premiums by reducing coverage. This works great only as long as you remain healthy, you say. My goal for you is to not only (1) reduce your cost of health care while you are healthy but also (2) when you have claims. After all, isn't that the point? Let us work together to keep as much money in your pocket as we can. The hospitals and insurance companies already get more than their fair share of the pot.

A Common Scenario (Demonstrating Application Of The HSA)

Mr. & Mrs. John and Jane Smith of Rochester Hills, MI: both 45 years of age and self-employed were paying $822 a month for their existing HMO plan. It had a $0 deductible, no co-insurance and $10 doctor visit co-pays. Prescriptions were not covered.

They replaced it with a $3000 family deductible HSA compatible plan that had a $554 a month premium. They made monthly deposits to their HSA account of $250. This amount, times 12 months, equaled $3000 deposited into their account and thus covered their deductible. This means they created a $0 deductible health plan for about the same dollar amount as their old plan. The difference between this plan and their old HMO is that the $3000 in the account is *theirs*. Unless they spend it on medical expenses, *they* keep the money, not the insurance company. Additionally, that money was deposited as pre-tax money for huge tax advantages. The money in an HSA rolls over year to year growing with interest, tax-deferred. Each year they can contribute from $1 to $5950 in pre-tax funds.

HSA vs. Old Traditional Insurance

Best Case Scenario (No health issues)

Deductible	$0	$0
Annual Premium	$9864	$6648
	———	———
Total Out-of Pocket	$9864	$6648 *Saves over $3000 plus tax benefits. Which is better?*

Worst Case Scenario (Serious health issues occur)

	Traditional	**HSA**
Deductible	$0	$3000
Annual Premium	$9864 ($822 X 12)	$6648 ($554 X 12)
	———	———
Total Out-of-Pocket	$9864	$9648 *Similar cost with better protection and tax benefits*

In the first year, John injures his knee and meets the deductible with surgery. $3000 is withdrawn from the account. Because the deductible has been met, both John and Jane have complete physicals and Jane opts for elective treatments to remove moles, a hemorrhoid and have a colonoscopy, all completely paid for by the plan. They pay $0 for all doctor visits and treatments.

When their policy has been in place for three years and they have over $6000 accumulated in their HSA fund, the Smiths decide to move to a higher deductible of $5900. This lowers their insurance premium by approximately $150 a month. They put the difference into their account, maximize their contribution and keep some of the money liquid with F.D.I.C. guaranteed interest and invest the remainder in Mutual Funds earning 7% interest, tax-deferred.

Each year they utilize the HSA account to pay a couple of hundred dollars on check ups and dental cleanings but otherwise remain relatively healthy other than two additional major claims by the time they retire. John and Jane pay the claims and still have nearly $100,000 in the HSA account to use in their retirement. **In the final analysis the Smiths get to keep the money that would have been profit for the insurance company.**

Securing The Best Healthcare Services Agent

<u>Three things you must know about the agent</u>
What to look for in an Agent:
1. Only deal with agents who are **local**, whom you can reach easily by telephone on Holidays and weekends.
2. Make sure your agent has great **ethics** in place, and will always do what is in your family's best interest.
3. Avoid the amateurs: deal with an agent who represents **several** firms, **knows all the plans** inside and out, and can bring you affordable **value**.

<u>Three questions you must ask to evaluate the policy</u>
What to look for in a Healthcare Services Firm:
1. Only deal with the top firms in the industry, 80 to 100-year-old firms with hundreds of millions of dollars in assets.
2. Ask what your **maximum out of pocket** (OOP) expense is.
3. Secure a high ($2 million +) lifetime maximum.

Exceptions: Why The HSA Is Not For Everyone
These are all False Assumptions.
1. You should only purchase an HSA if you are healthy and don't expect to have claims.
2. You should not purchase an HSA if you have pre-existing health issues and need to see a doctor regularly.

3. You should not purchase an HSA if you are a family with very young children who go to the doctor often.

While these circumstances might indicate that you may be accessing your account more often, in most circumstances you will still be ahead financially. Do not accept a general statement that an HSA is not for you until a cost analysis has been done.

Some Cautionary Words Of Advice

Let us look at the traditional low-deductible plan you currently have. Do you really have what you think you purchased? Hopefully your old agent had your family's best interest at heart when he sold you your previous plan. After all, you only had to pay a small co-pay the last time you were feeling achy and needed an antibiotic. But, do you know how your policy is going to hold up when something really serious happens? The time to find out your coverage is limited in any usual and likely situation is not when you already have filed a major claim. There are more than 25 insurance companies operating here in Michigan. Most of them do a great job in protecting you. Some popular insurance companies have fine print in their policy that could leave you the client on the hook over critical issues if you don't take the necessary steps to correct them. Take your policy out. Read it. Yes, the legalese is difficult to read. The average layman might skim over the policy, miss a key sentence or two and not realize that an important issue is not covered. **Find an experienced benefit advisor who knows the plans inside and out.** One who is concerned for your best interest and who will review your policy at no obligation and make you aware of any issues.

Brief Biographical Notes

Let me share some professional details so that you can place this information in perspective. I have a BFA in Commercial Photography from the College for Creative Studies. For nearly 10 years, I owned and operated a successful commercial photography studio specializing in industrial and advertising photography. In 2002, as the industry changed with the advent of digital processes, I changed direction to help people with solutions for their health insurance problems. I am now one of five Senior Partners of a firm headquartered in Waterford, Michigan called CBI Agency. (Incidentally, CBI stands for **"Client's Best Interest"**). I have helped thousands of individuals, families, small business owners and the self-employed obtain low cost, high quality Health, Life and Disability Insurance when they are either not eligible for or can't afford large group coverage. I work with the client to customize the plan and shop the market to find the best value. You the client can select from top A-rated insurance companies such as Blue Cross/Blue Shield of Michigan to privately held PPOM firms such as World, United Health Care, Assurant and American Community. With nearly 20 companies to choose from, the client has versatility in selecting and often even combining companies to provide the best possible protection.

Final Recommendations

Set an appointment with a qualified benefit advisor to obtain the information to make an informed purchase. Disregard any initial concerns of the higher family deductible and look at the bigger picture of total out-of-pocket expense with and without claims. In so doing the advantages will be clear.

HSAs are government legislated programs. Regardless of the carrier, the program has to fit IRS guidelines to qualify for the tax advantages. The benefit to you is that a future move from one carrier to another can be made with the confidence that coverage will be comparable on an apples-to-apples basis. This allows you to shop the market if and when your program experiences an increase in premium or a decrease in customer satisfaction. This acts as a self-regulating safeguard against unusually high rates and insures that the market will remain competitive for you to get a good value.

You can rest easy knowing that you made the right decision for your family's health care not only for the present but for the long term.

> *I recently worked with Keith Parke to address a concern I have had for several years. My health insurance had been increasing every year and the coverage was just so so. My family needed the coverage, but finding the right person to come up with a plan to reduce cost for good coverage was far and few between.*
>
> *I finally met Keith Parke through a networking event and we followed up to see if there was anything that could be done to reduce my current coverage and at a minimum, maintain the benefits of the current insurance. Once we did a side by side analysis of features for coverage with a proposed plan, we found that a plan for less monthly cost with increased coverage was achievable.*
>
> *We decided to change over to this new plan since it made sense on two fronts, reduced cost of premiums and increased health benefits coverage.*
>
> DAVID BANET, Troy, Michigan

About the Author:

Keith Parke is a senior partner at CBI Agency located in Waterford, MI. You can reach him at (248) 840-0911 for a free evaluation of your current policy.

Keith Parke
CBI Agency
1370 N. Oakland Blvd.
Suite 120
Waterford, MI 48327

Cell (248) 840-0911
Office (866) 488-2603
Fax (248) 666-5300
kparke@cbiagency.net
www.cbiagency.net

Why Your Father's Retirement Plan Won't Work For You

By Sandra Wright with Minesh Baxi

The most urgent question people have in planning their retirement years is - will I outlive my money?

This is partly because one of the biggest challenges people have today in planning their retirement is due to lack of viable plans which took care of the previous generation.

Maybe your parents worked at a big corporation with generous pension plans and they could spend their retirements in relative comfort without too many worries.

This is no longer the case.

You should be aware of the fact that we have seen huge changes in the retirement planning for the current generation and beyond. These changes should make you more focused and committed to evaluate the best options for your retirement future.

Our purpose is to make sure you understand the need for retirement planning and why it is different from that of previous generations.

Here are a few reasons why your father's retirement plan cannot be your retirement plan.

1. **Lack Of Pensions**: There was a time when a portion of an employee's paycheck was used to fund a pension plan also called defined benefit plan. At the time of retirement, the employee got a decent remuneration to last his/her lifetime.

The pension benefit depended on the type of corporation and the amount of the paycheck. In most cases these employees had little or no concern about funding their own pension plan and planning for their retirement apart from the company pension plan.

With changing times, such plans have become less and less common. Even big companies like GM, Ford and Chrysler no longer provide such generous plans.

There are quite a few reasons that this is not viable for many corporations and employees are ill-advised to look for such plans.

Here are a few reasons why and we will elaborate later:

a. People are living much longer and the pension funds cannot continue pay outs for these longer durations.

b. Fast rising health care costs have forced companies to separate pension plans and health care benefits. Previously, a pension included health care benefits. That is not prevalent any longer as companies cannot take on this unknown future liability.

c. Companies going out of business has been another reason that the pension plans are no longer available. The incident of Eastern Airlines is a well-documented example of employees and retirees left with substantially reduced or no pensions despite the promises made by the company.

d. Underfunded Pension Fund Liability: This is basically one of the most gruesome facts about pension funds. Companies have been permitted to borrow from their pension funds to pay for their capital and operating expenses. In quite a few cases the companies have declared the pension funds bankrupt and there is no recourse for the employee.

These are just some of the reasons why employees can no longer expect to participate in pension plans from their organizations to take care of them during the retirement years.

There is an exception and those are the government-sponsored pension plans. Government employees typically enjoy the best pension plans and quite often if the government cannot fund it – they have an easy method of raising taxes to keep paying their employees and retirees.

This has been an attractive feature of government jobs and as the private sector shifts more and more of the responsibility for retirement to the individual employee, quite a few people may want to work for the public sector.

2. Rising Health Care Costs: This is one of the biggest reasons that a retirement plan made just a few years ago cannot support the individual or the family today. There is no way that this trend is going downward. There is a lot of talk of Universal Health Care. The issue that most people do not realize is that there will need to be higher taxes to pay for this program. Higher taxes will leave people with even less money to fund their own retirement plan.

Currently, the total average annual cost for family coverage premiums is $12,106. That is a sizeable sum surpassing the social security benefits for most people over 65 years.

This makes it essential to plan for such increases in your retirement plan.

3. Government Inspired 401K Plans Did Not Exist: It was not until the 1970's that the 401 K type tax-deferred plans came into existence. These plans have dramatically altered the landscape of retirement planning. Almost all financial advisors recommend using 401 K, 403B, IRAs, Roth IRAs etc to fund the retirement plans.

There are two reasons:

    a. Today it is a lot easier to control and manage these funds and create a mixed portfolio of different stock and other investments.

    b. Organizations have shifted the responsibility of taking care of their retirement years to the employees and made this plan more attractive by offering matching contributions. This has practically antiquated the practice of pensions.

4. We Are Living Too Long: Nobody really feels that he or she is living too long. However long we live, we will feel that maybe we could live longer and possibly healthier thanks to advances in medical technology.

In just over a hundred years we have increased the average life span in the USA from about 47 years to 77 years. At no point in the human civilization did the life-span grow so fast!

Obviously it is a big positive that people can enjoy their children, grandchildren and even great grandchildren. Unfortunately, it has a disadvantageous side as well. People wish to retire as early in their lives as possible so they can have more fun during the golden years.

The question is, who will fund these long golden years?

Though people continue to be quite productive even in their seventies, most people do not feel the urge or have the energy to hold down a full-time job during this time.

In some cases, failing health prevents them from working long hours to support their lifestyle. All this means that people's retirement plans are more likely to run out of money sooner than they would prefer.

This is another reason that your retirement plan needs more fine-tuning and more detailed forecasting than might have been the case just a few years ago.

5. Social Security Is Going Bankrupt: Despite all the promises by politicians, the fact is that the current social security system is on its way to becoming bankrupt. Politicians are poor money managers and their focus is just getting elected or re-elected. They have no desire to tackle difficult issues and there are very few leaders in politics.

Most politicians are power-hungry opportunists and have very little or no interest in solving any problems. If we sound cynical, it is to ask you to not depend on any politician to help you. You are much better off planning outside the government domain.

Even if the social security can pay you an amount at retirement, it is unlikely that it will be adequate to take care of your lifestyle.

6. We Want A Better Lifestyle In Retirement: golfing and traveling. Today's retirees are not invalids sitting on their porches or just watching TV all day long. Today's retirees want to stay active engaging in volunteering, sports and recreations like golfing and traveling. Needless to say that these hobbies require more money. Planning for future needs based on minimum expenses will not suffice for this ambitious generation.

Again, why settle for less? You worked hard to become free of your daily work obligations, why not take time to travel to the ruins of Rome, watch Wimbledon Tennis live or enjoy the symphony at the New York Philharmonic?

7. There Are More Options To Create The Wealth: This may sound contrary to most of the doom and gloom reports but the fact is that there are abundant opportunities to create wealth today. Look at companies such as Microsoft, Dell, Yahoo and Google. These companies have been literally overnight successes. The founders of these companies became billionaires and continue to dominate the Forbes Richest lists.

What does that have to do with you? You do not have to start another Google!

However, having invested smartly, you could have made a lot more money as well. With the advancement of internet and communications it is faster to get your product, service or just an idea to millions of people worldwide much faster. You could become famous very quickly and you could cash in on the new-found fame.

It is not our intention to explore this option here but you must take heart and look for opportunities to create more wealth which can sustain your lifestyle in the golden years which could still be productive years.

8. Expectations And Needs Are Different:
What people expect from their retirement years and investments has changed significantly in recent years.

9. Companies/Stocks Which Were Considered Good Buys Are No Longer Good Buys:
There was a time when the advice was to buy good stocks and hold them through thick and thin. It did not matter whether you were in a bearish or a bullish market, you could ride out the ups and downs and eventually come out ahead.

Unfortunately with the volatile markets upon us, it is no longer possible to wait for the tide to turn in your favor. It is highly recommended that you stay close to the information about the market and make sure that you are not holding stocks of companies which have gone bankrupt or are likely to do so.

Stock prices can come down very fast and if you are not prepared or not looking after your assets, you could be in for a rude awakening. We all know people who bought stocks during the Tech boom in the 1990's and put all their eggs in one basket. Some people woke up to discover that they will have to find work to pay for their basic needs in the so-called retirement years.

10. Not Same Long Term Stability In Stock Dividends: Stock dividends have gone down to typically 2% a year. This amount does not keep in line with inflation, let alone handle your lifestyle.

11. You Have To Keep Up With Changes: Your plan could be totally different 10 years from now. Life brings about changes anyway. It is imperative that you keep evaluating your needs and modify the plan based on any changes that may take place, foreseen or unforeseen.

12. There Are Very Few Guarantees: There are only two guarantees: taxes and death. There are very few guarantees then how do you plan? Very carefully! You cannot let your eyes off the ball and you must pay attention to your changing environment and your needs.

About the Authors:

Sandra Wright has managed and run a number of successful businesses. She also helps manage a multi-million dollar portfolio for her family. She is currently authoring a book "*Investment Secret Of The Rich*" (www.InvestmentSecretOfTheRich.com)

Minesh Baxi is successful co-author of "*Network Your Way To $100,000 And Beyond*" and "*Stop Hiring Losers*". Minesh helps businesses create the competitive edge by becoming known as an expert by creating information products like Audio CDs, DVD and books along with web presence.

To get your free audio CD "*7 Ways To Be Recognized As The Expert*" call 877-968-2500 or email minesh@mbaxi.com.

A Contingency Plan – The "Do Or Die" Safety Net For Business Owners

By Pat Byrd

Owning and managing a business can be a daunting, complex and difficult process. Overseeing a business operation on a day-to-day basis takes persistence, diligence, a major investment of time and money, knowledge of basic business principles and the availability of resources – to name a few. Nothing helps to keep operations flowing more smoothly than a good, sound contingency plan.

What is a Contingency Plan?

A contingency plan is comprised of strategies and mini-action plans which create remedies for a specific situation when things go wrong. It helps anticipate problems well before they occur, establishes a game plan for "what ifs", and is a safety net to help people that have to work under the plan.

A contingency plan is sometimes called a "back-up plan", "worst-case scenario" or "Plan B". The strategies could be:
- simple steps describing what to do during a short period of downtime,
- shifting the direction of your business model if market trends are changing, or
- ultimately, selling the business outright using an "exit strategy".

Contingency plans are the "saving grace" to help a business recover from minor situations or even serious incidents within a minimum amount of time, cost and disruption.

Why Should You Have One and What Will Happen If You Don't?

A contingency plan can lead to a better use of manpower and resources and is built on protecting the assets of a business. It allows the smart business owner to build a hedge against failure and be secure in the knowledge that things can be put back on track quickly.

Contingency plans are often developed to prepare for any eventuality during times of crisis. The importance of proper planning for "what ifs" cannot be over-emphasized. It is quite obvious that FEMA, the Executive Office of the U.S. government, the governmental bodies of Louisiana and other southern and southwestern states affected in 2005 by Hurricane Katrina were not prepared with a good contingency plan for a large-scale crisis. To make matters worse, they did not have an effective disaster recovery plan, and other areas hit by Hurricane Ike are now being affected some three years later.

The very process of contingency planning can get an entire organization to think more positive about the importance of various business systems. Within the past 75 to 100 years, the importance of contingency planning has been underscored. For an example, contingency plans are used by quality-driven organizations to effectively deal with the rapidly-changing technology environment.

Remedies to Consider When Emergencies Arise or Market Trends Change

- Keep Your Cool. Being nervous, anxious and uncomfortable when things go wrong is normal, but the key is to not allow emergency conditions to prevent you from doing your best. Be well prepared – being anxious can prevent you from demonstrating your expertise and launching your contingency plan.

- Create Worst Case Scenarios. List your worst fears and bad things you think might happen. Envision yourself in each of these situations. Envision challenges that could happen, and create logical steps on paper for your recovery plan so that it makes sense. Go through practical steps of rehearsals, and get feedback from others – as they will probably think of things you may have overlooked.

- Be Time Efficient. Plan what needs to be done and said in as little time as necessary. Always have a back-up supply of materials, equipment, machinery and other resources – whatever is needed to continue the operation of your business for a specific period of time.

- Be Ready for Questions. Think of as many questions ahead of time that may develop in a crisis that could come from your clients or employees – then create logical responses that make sense. Sometimes people create more problems during a crisis because they invent fake answers. It may be better to say "I don't know at this moment, but I'll get back with you quickly on that."

- Stay Informed. Keep up with what is going on in your particular line of business – technologically, financially, and marketwise – and keep abreast of the trends for the future of your business model. Involve the appropriate people by asking questions and talking about your business with experts and external consultants.

- Be Ready to Change. Sometimes, conditions can develop that are so severe that you have to change your business model altogether. It can be said that "change" is like letting go of one trapeze in the air in order to catch the next one. For a small amount of time, it may be like holding on to nothing but thin air. But catching the next trapeze can get you to a new platform and a new place. Invite ideas, experiment and interview those who are successful or have pulled off changes.

- Involve Your Stakeholders. If your business has stakeholders, your contingency plan should include marketing strategies to maintain their support and understanding. Stakeholders need to be kept informed of the reasons for any changes, the vision of the end result and the proposed game plan to get there. If it makes sense, garner input from the most influential stakeholders – without acceptance from them, any plan may encounter limited success.

- Develop Exit Strategies. On the far end of the spectrum is the option of developing an exit strategy if you determine that the best way out of your business is to sell it. Various reasons exist for exit strategies to be developed – retirement, illness of an owner, plans to relocate to another state or country, personal issues (such as a pending divorce). Plan the implementation of an exit strategy well in advance as it is just as important as how the business was started.

Steps for Creating a Contingency Plan

Contingency plans can range from very simple to complex and should be designed based on an organization's needs. The contingency planning process should include the following elements:

- List every process in the company – if you have departments, list each departmental process.
- List the tasks for every process – then list the steps it takes to complete each task.
- List every dependency for every step (computer hardware, software, external and internal suppliers, supplies, equipment, etc.).
- Assume that every dependency will fail – then rate and prioritize the possibility for failure.
- Write a contingency action that accomplishes the task without relying upon the dependency.

Once you have analyzed business functions this way, you should be able to create contingencies for the various processes that keep your business up and running.

Structure your contingency plan with a positive atmosphere, and involve the appropriate people and the right amount of people. After all – it's a big task. It will require input from many.

Test Your Contingency Plan

Trying to test every facet in your plan can be prohibitive of time and costs. To make testing manageable, test your plan in four stages with each stage building on the results of the previous stage. If an area proves to be unsound or conflicts with other parts of your plan, you can always re-write and re-test that part of the plan.

Stage 1 - Senior Executive Staff Review

The senior executive staff should select an internally-publicized date and time to review all contingency plans. This review serves to recognize people who have thoughtfully completed their assignment as well as to ensure overall business soundness.

Stage 2 - Interdepartmental Reviews

If your business has departments, each department should review another department's plans. Example: departments that are "downstream" in the business process can review the plans of "upstream" departments. The purpose of this stage is to find bottlenecks, identify conflicts and allocate resources, if necessary.

Stage 3 - Failures in Critical Systems

This testing should be localized within departments and involves simulating system or vendor failures. Critical equipment or processes do not have to actually be shut down – "what if" scenarios can be put into action. A role-playing event can be scheduled for a specific time.

Stage 4 – Testing "The Real Deal"

Testing involves short-term shutdowns in key areas. If possible, these tests should be conducted in a real-time environment – not after most employees have left for the day. The goal, of course, is to fully test components of the contingency plan. Concentrate this last phase of testing only on areas that have a high business priority and a high risk for failure.

By implementing the testing in four stages, you can optimize your time and accomplish the goal of proving that the contingency plan works.

The Exit Strategy

In business, an exit strategy, exit plan, or strategic withdrawal can be a way to either discontinue the operation of some part of the company or to terminate ownership of the company ("cash out"). It may include an initial public offering (IPO) or being bought out by a larger player in the industry.

Personal Experience

I have first-hand knowledge of the critical importance of creating an effective contingency plan and actually putting the plan into action. These 20 years of business ownership have encompassed a variety of service and product offerings to a diverse client base. At B2B Funding, LLC, our services are provided nationwide to religious entities and non-profit organizations to secure funding for mortgage and construction loans and asset-based financing. These services are provided in conjunction with my collaborative partner of five years – the Office of the Ecclesiastical Council.

With the current downturn of the economy, our clients have frequently been disappointed with the decline of market values of their commercial properties and other assets – sometimes as low as 50% compared to just two or three years ago. In addition, some lenders have gone out of business due to these tough economic times and have thereby limited access to the funding required to support our clients. These conditions have adversely affected the financial stability of our clients and have had a huge impact on our cash flow.

Developing a contingency plan was one of the smartest moves we could have made. Our survival is based on strategies and relationships that were developed two years ago – which, at that time, were created to expand our offerings – but are now being used to resuscitate our future. In addition to continuing the work of our current clientele, we have recently become the advisory consultants and training team to an international organization that grants funding to grassroots, faith-based, community services organizations. By creating contingency plans during a time our main source of business was thriving, we now have strategies to rely on, to sustain us and to keep growing.

Summary

While creating and testing contingency plans may seem like a time-consuming, non-value-added investment of resources, it has the potential to create positive change within a company. When people take a closer look at the every day assumptions pertaining to their work and ask a variety of "what if"-type questions, the results often lead to more efficient processes. Remember – the Chinese symbol for "crisis" and "opportunity" are the same.

About the Author:

Patricia Byrd is founder of B2B Funding, LLC, located in Southfield, Michigan. Feel free to contact her at (248) 827-9684, by email at MoneyLady@B2BFundingLLC.com or at www.OECouncil.org.

What's The Enemy: Spending More Or Spending Less On Employee Benefits
(How To Retain Your Best Employees Without Spending A Fortune)
By Ted Himelhoch and Martyn Dickinson

In 1887, Edward Bellamy wrote in "Looking Backward," "The relation between the workingman and the employer, between labor and capital, appeared in some unaccountable manner to have become dislocated." How little has changed since 1887 for one of the greatest problems facing the United States today is the rising cost of employee benefits. Behind this issue is the lack of understanding of how to contain those costs and make them a profitable cost and the further erosion of the employee/employer relationship because of this development. Employers have trended toward shrinking health benefits as well as shifting the burden of paying for the plan to the employee to contain the cost of the plans. Therefore, to the employee, healthcare costs feel like they are skyrocketing while the benefits are reduced and some are stealing from their retirement savings to pay the additional costs.

The problem of increasing costs of benefits is just as difficult for the employer. They see the benefit costs spiraling out of control and feel powerless to do anything about it except to react as best they can. Thus far this has meant sharing the increase with the employee. So the problem will likely continue to worsen for several reasons:

First, health care costs are projected to continue to increase and the premiums will do the same unless alternative plans are utilized which could reduce these costs. Employee stress is increasing dramatically due to the increased cost of coverage.

Second, employees are decreasing contributions to their retirement plans and reducing discretionary spending to cover the increasing costs (Ameriprise Study, 2007).

Third, the stress then steals work time. Employees use time
at work to try to solve the additional problems created by the
increased costs.

If this trend continues, we have a lose-lose situation for the
employer, the employee and the relationship between the two.
Employers are likely to have a victim mentality due to the fear of the
economy. They have seen their only out as passing on the increased
health care costs to the employee because they see this as more cost
effective. But in reality, this approach may be a myth. Employers
could actually see increases in costs due to lower productivity of the
workers and losing higher qualified workers to companies that still
provide full benefit programs. Companies may face higher costs
overall because employees feel no loyalty and come and go. So the
cost of rehiring and retraining employees is outweighing the benefit
the business sees by turning over the increased health care cost to
those same workers.

How the authors see the problem

A suitable solution to this problem demands an understanding of the
unique challenges faced by each group, employees and employers.
Once that understanding is achieved, it becomes possible to review
the applicable regulations and to define a frame work for the
solution. The next stage is to develop strategies making best use of
the appropriate financial products available in the market place. In
writing this chapter we have therefore reviewed a range of articles and
research papers, the most prominent being those listed at the end.
Following that review, we believe that a two-stage solution is called
for which will allow employers to get back to offering diverse benefit
packages which, in turn, will see their companies full of happier,
healthier and more motivated employees.

Stage One – High Deductible Healthcare Plans and Health Savings Accounts

First, we recommend that employers address the healthcare issue by considering the use of new health care insurance programs to replace what are perceived as the tried and true plans that are now in place at most businesses. These traditional co-pay and low deductible plans continue to put more money in the insurance companies' pockets from higher premiums but, unfortunately, many employees in these plans do not fully utilize the benefits. So why not begin to look more thoroughly at High Deductible Health Plans (HDHPs) which if they meet certain IRS requirements, allow individuals to open Health Savings Accounts (HSAs).

Many employers have looked at HDHPs with HSAs but do not embrace their benefits. They believe these plans will cost more and that the employees will not accept them. However, we believe this is unlikely to be the case, especially if employers and employees have a good understanding of how the plans can work as a long term strategy and not just on an annual basis.

A recognized fear is that because of the higher deductible, employees will not utilize the plan. This has happened with some high deductible plans, but we believe that has occurred because the plans were not implemented with the necessary education and subsequent understanding of how best to utilize the benefits of the high deductible plan. Also, research shows most employees and their families will not spend a lot on health care during the course of a given year. For those who do; their total costs will be very similar whether in a traditional plan or a high deductible plan. For the majority who will not spend much out-of-pocket, the savings on premiums can now be used to fund their Health Savings Accounts. Assuming that individuals actually contribute their premium savings into their HSA and do not incur significant out of pocket medical expenses, the account balance should begin to build and within a couple years they should have more than enough to cover the high deductible. Imagine that after two years of contributing premium savings to an HSA, many employees may have as much as $2,000-$6,000 in their Health Savings Accounts to pay for deductibles and other out of pocket expenses.

Stage Two – Providing employee education through a workplace financial planning provider.

Now that we have started to beat the drum on education we come to stage two of the solution. There has been a trend over recent years for businesses to place more responsibility for saving for retirement and paying for healthcare in the hands of the individual without adequately addressing the educational needs of the employee. Recent studies have shown that American employees are ready to meet the challenge of this increased responsibility but are also looking to their employers to provide the necessary financial education to help them make sound, informed choices. Indeed, there may be a direct correlation between the willingness of employers to provide that education and the loyalty of their employees. Employers can add educational benefits that provide added value geared toward attracting and retaining the highest quality employee at zero or minimal additional cost. A good example of this is workplace financial planning, a service offered by some financial planning companies.

Here is how it works. The employer establishes a business arrangement with a workplace financial planning provider. The Provider works with the Human Resources department to learn and understand their benefits program and then uses that knowledge to provide education to employees in the form of seminars, workshops and written materials. Education can be on a range of financial topics including how the benefits program functions regarding health insurance and saving for retirement and how best to leverage it. Education can be most effective when specifically targeted, based on the demographics and needs of the workforce. The Provider can also be the first point of contact for benefit questions. The benefits of workplace financial planning to the employer can include:
- A better informed, less financially stressed and more satisfied employee who is less likely to seek employment elsewhere.
- A Human Resources department with more time to concentrate on other HR issues.

The workplace financial planning relationship can be as simple or as in-depth as the employer chooses. It may involve basic education regarding the company benefits package to employees at a group level, through to more individualized, comprehensive financial help with an employee's complete financial picture. Whilst there are generally costs for this level of service, they can be reduced by economies of scale. Studies have shown that many employees are looking for this level of one-on-one financial education and guidance in their benefits package. Often the employee may pay the reduced cost in full or the employer may decide to use savings made elsewhere to subsidize a portion of the cost of the financial planning.

Win-win-win scenario

We believe this to be a win-win-win scenario:

- The employee wins by having a thorough understanding of the benefit choices available (and at what cost), greater control of costs, and the opportunity to use comprehensive financial planning at a discount.
- The employer wins in two ways: by having a more stable workforce less likely to be distracted by benefits issues and more likely to stay with the organization, and by having a Human Resources department which can concentrate on other important HR issues.
- The workplace financial planning provider wins by having a long term financial planning relationship with educated, motivated individuals with a commitment to their financial well-being.

Looking Forward?

So, 120 years after the publication of "Looking Backward" are Edward Bellamy's observations on the relationship between the working man and the employer still valid? Studies suggest that the provision of a comprehensive benefits package, including targeted education, will continue to be an important factor in that relationship. However, there is still an important perception gap with regard to employee loyalty and the role played by benefits. For example a 2008 Met Life study showed that 81% of employees saw healthcare benefits as an important factor in workforce loyalty; only 60% of employers agreed. 72% of employees saw retirement benefits as an important loyalty factor; only 41% of employers agreed.

The 2007 Ameriprise Financial Benefits study found that 83% of workers indicated that it was moderately or very important that they feel valued by their employer through the benefits offered in the workplace. Additionally, 70% of employees indicated that they would be moderately or very interested in one-on-one financial advice if offered through their employer.

Let's summarize:

- Financial stress has increased over recent years as employees have taken on greater responsibility for their healthcare and retirement funding decisions.
- Employees are willing to meet the challenge but need good financial education to help them make wise choices.
- As those choices become more complex, employees can benefit from more individualized education and advice.
- Employers can provide that education and advice with workplace financial planning agreements at zero to minimal cost, reducing financial stress, retaining good employees and ultimately helping to maintain or improve the employer's bottom line.

In our view the message is clear. Employers who want to attract and retain the best employees need a comprehensive, targeted benefits package that includes sound financial education. The resources now exist to help them achieve it.

About the Authors:

Ted N Himelhoch, CRPC®
Senior Financial Advisor
Ameriprise Financial Services, Inc.
269-323-1100

N Martyn Dickinson, CRPC®
Associate Financial Advisor

Additional sources:

The 2007 Ameriprise Workplace Financial Planning Benefit Decisions Study — www.ameriprise.com/global/docs/pr-benefits.pdf

Milliman Research Report - Consumer Driven Impact Study, April 2008 — www.milliman.com/expertise/healthcare/publications/rr/pdfs/consumer-driven-impact-studyRR-04-01-08.pdf

Met Life – Sixth Annual Study of Employee Benefit Trends — www.whymetlife.com/trends/index.asp

Met Life - The 2008 Study of the American Dream — www.metlife.com/Applications/Corporate/WPS/CDA/PageGenerator/0,,p14305,00.html

Employee Benefit Research Institute (EBRI) Issue Brief No 312, December 2007 - The Future of Employment-Based Health Benefits: Have Employers Reached a Tipping Point? — www.ebri.org/publications/ib/index. cfm?fa=ibDisp&content id=3868

BONUS SECTION:
Makeover Success Stories from Chambers/Associations

Jennifer Kluge, COO, Michigan Business Owners and Professionals Association

Jennifer Kluge is a visionary. As the COO of Michigan Business Owners and Professionals Association and the publisher of CORP! Magazine, she has seen personally what it takes to be an entrepreneur.

MBPA has over 20,000 members and provides the required support to its members. Her staff is willing to help any member and they are only a phone call away.

When she took on the CORP! Magazine, the magazine had stopped publishing but the idea was there. She saw the potential to sell the good news despite the naysayers. Today CORP! has a readership of over 37,000 in the state of Michigan.

How did she help create that business makeover?

Jennifer says- Success in business is 100% dependent on your attitude.

It can be lonely as an entrepreneur and that is why the CORP! Magazine has attracted people who are seeking positive reinforcement, ideas and successful people to network with learn from. By hosting events to recognize and elevate best practices, Jennifer and her team have created the positive buzz in the area to counteract the doom and gloom which people can easily fall prey to. She firmly believes that "Good news can sell."

Jennifer knows what it takes to be successful in business. Her secret is to be an active listener to her clients and her team. By being tuned into what is happening into the marketplace, she has pioneered various successful projects. CORP! is an example of such a project.

Her message to entrepreneurs is simple:
a. Work hard
b. Listen to the marketplace
c. Try different approaches, constantly think of yourself as a new CEO and be flexible

d. Communicate, communicate, communicate with employees and clients

e. Persevere because there is no such thing as an overnight success

Jennifer Kluge can be reached at (586) 393-8800 or visit http://www.michbusiness.org

Sheri Heiney, Executive Director, Rochester Regional Chamber of Commerce

When Sheri Heiney took on the role of the Executive Director of Rochester Chamber of Commerce, the chamber had just over 600 members. Just 5 years later the chamber boasts of 1400 members. Congratulations to Sheri and her team for receiving Outstanding Chamber of the Year Award in the large category for the state of Michigan for 2008!

Here are four principles which govern her success:

1. **Fresh perspective**: Sheri was an outsider to the Rochester area with fresh eyes. Based on her interview, the Board realized that Sheri could see the negatives as well as the positives in the community and bring about the much needed change.

2. **Be an investigator**: Sheri was very willing to listen and learn from the people who had lived in the area for a while as well as held responsible positions and contributed to the community. She identified the key customers and leaders and sought their opinion. She found out that there were challenges simmering to a point that it was a possibility that Rochester Hills might be creating its own chamber instead of remaining with the Rochester Regional Chamber.

3. **Put together a comprehensive three year business plan**: The chamber revised its mission statement and by brainstorming with capable people, designed the new look and feel, creating a vibrant image.

4. **Don't focus on just membership dues to sustain the chamber:** Sheri realized early on that if the chamber had to be financially viable, she needed to seek more opportunities

to raise funds and not just focus on membership dues. With numerous events and sponsorship opportunities for businesses in the area, the chamber has been able to provide the much needed exposure for businesses while keeping the chamber financially healthy.

You can reach Sheri Heiney at (248) 651-6700. The chamber website is www.rrc-mi.com

Penny Shanks Executive Director, Clarkston Area Chamber of Commerce

To break membership record in 2008 during the economic slowdown in Michigan is truly amazing! That is exactly what Penny and her hard working staff have accomplished. Penny Shanks has been the backbone of the Clarkston Area Chamber of Commerce for so many years that one cannot imagine how it would be like without her.

Here are some of her secrets to success:

1. **Leading by example**: Penny is planning to run a marathon for her 50th birthday in Disneyworld®. Her commitment has inspired numerous people. She brings the same dedication and commitment to her role as the Chamber Executive Director.

2. **Smart hiring and delegation**: Penny has the knack of finding the right people for the job and then helping them succeed. Her team is always eager to do whatever it takes to get the job done.

3. **Keeping the pulse on the market**: By surveying her community, Penny has been able to identify needs of various businesses. She helps B2B and B2C members with events that support them.

4. **Implementing the vision with the Board of Directors**: Penny knows that she must work cohesively with the members of the Board to create a strategic vision and then find partners to help make that happen. All the members love working with her.

5. **Very approachable**: Penny has created an open door policy with her members and staff so you can feel assured that she will listen to you and help you to her best ability.

Penny Shanks can be reached at 248-625-8055. You can find out more about the chamber at www.clarkston.org

Marie Hauswirth, Executive Director, Waterford Area Chamber of Commerce

When Marie took over the Waterford Area Chamber of Commerce, it was struggling to get members and provide services to the community. Today the chamber is a thriving group of enthusiastic members who have forged a strong bond creating a vibrant community.

Here are five keys to Marie's success:

1. Marie brings with her experience from non-profit, corporate and small business sectors. This has helped her to understand the needs of a small business owner and the needs of the community as well. She knows the hard work and risks included in owning a business.
2. Focusing on the pain: Marie learned long time ago from the Sandler Sales System to find the pain of the customer. That is why she is good at finding and alleviating the pain of the members.
3. B2B and B2C businesses have different needs: Marie has created programs, ongoing education and marketing opportunities for her B2B and B2C clients. She provides affordable, targeted marketing solutions through the chamber services.
4. Create successful matchmaking partnerships: Marie believes it is all about building relationships that can help the chamber and its members. Recently Clarkston and Waterford chamber conducted numerous events like Business over breakfast and small business seminar.
5. Make the community a great place to be: At the heart of all of this is Marie's passion for making Waterford area the place to

be for businesses and people alike. She lives in the area and is committed to help people prosper together.

Marie can be reached at 248-666-8600 or you can visit http://www.waterfordchamber.org

Mailè Ilac Boeder, Executive Director Ferndale Chamber of Commerce

In the last 3 years Mailè has seen numerous changes in the area and she has been on the forefront of leading the charge of making the chamber more flexible so it can meet the demands of its members. Mailè believes in going the distance. Here are some of the major changes she has instituted to help her members:

1. Provide networking opportunities morning, noon and night so businesses can meet other businesses when it is convenient for them
2. A website that is updated weekly so people can find businesses and businesses can locate useful information about the chamber along with email newsletters
3. The Chamber is open 6 days a week to accommodate the busy schedule of its members. In fact the chamber is open till 8 pm on Thursdays
4. The chamber even has a Facebook page and has acquired members by using the social media. The chamber will help people set up on different social media marketing sites like LinkedIn, MySpace and Facebook.
5. Mailè's staff hand addresses envelopes. This is to make the member feel special and let them know that the staff values the members. This is almost unheard of in today's busy world.
6. Mailè takes her time to meet with businesses and gives them 30 minutes of her time to see of there is anything she can do to assist in helping with issues with the city or just to make better business decisions.

7. The chamber surveys its members regularly using the phone to offer that personal touch.

8. Like the Verizon® commercial, this is a network you can count on.

You can reach Mailè Ilac Boeder at (248) 542-2160 or you can visit www.ferndalechamber.com

Meet all the experts from this book at
www.30DayTotalBusinessMakeover.com

We have numerous resources for you:

a. Articles from the authors &

b. Special offers for your business

**Do you want to be a published author to
attract more and better clients?**

Get your free CD

"7 Ways To Be Recognized As The Expert"

and a complimentary book coaching session

at www.30DayTotalBusinessMakeover.com